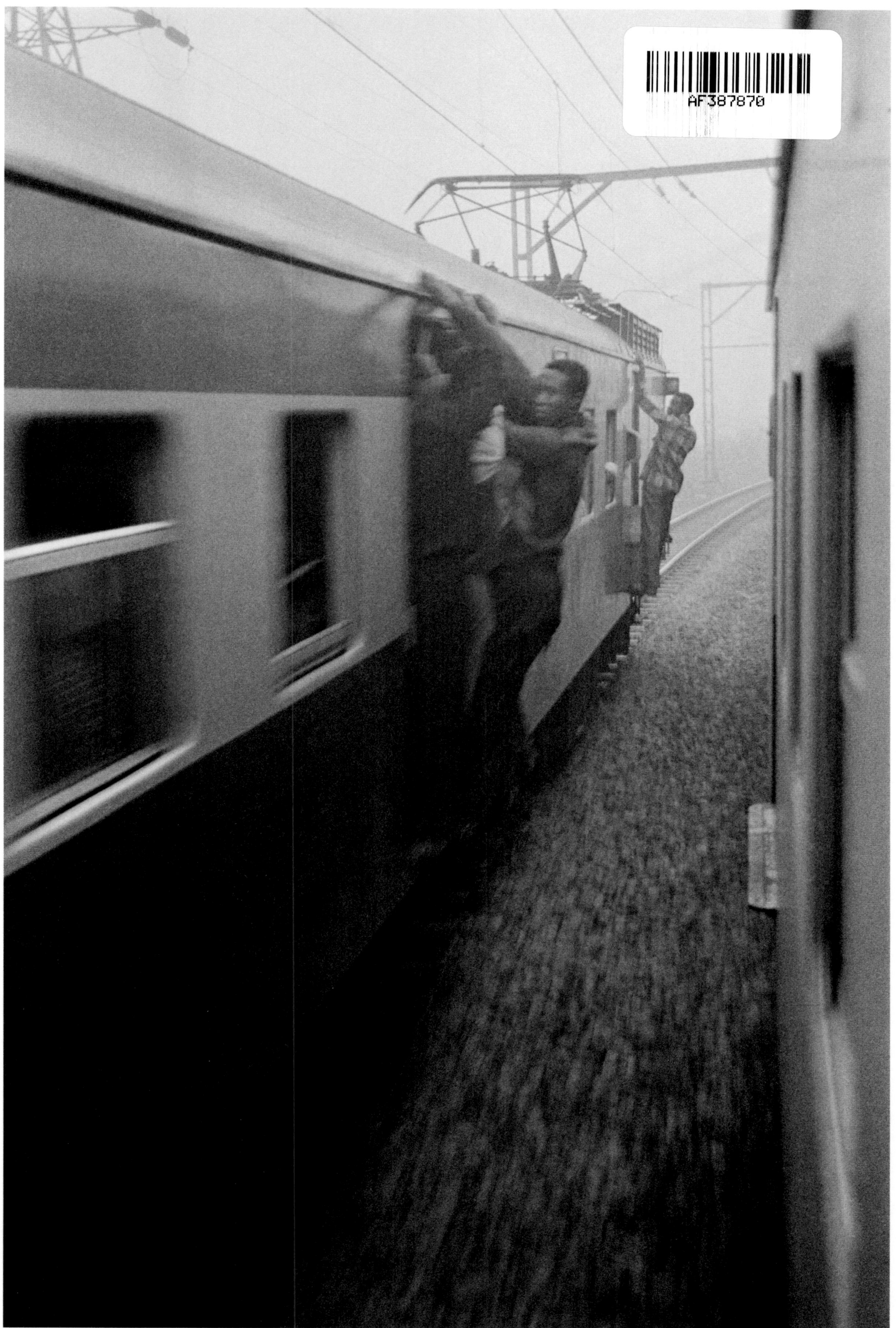

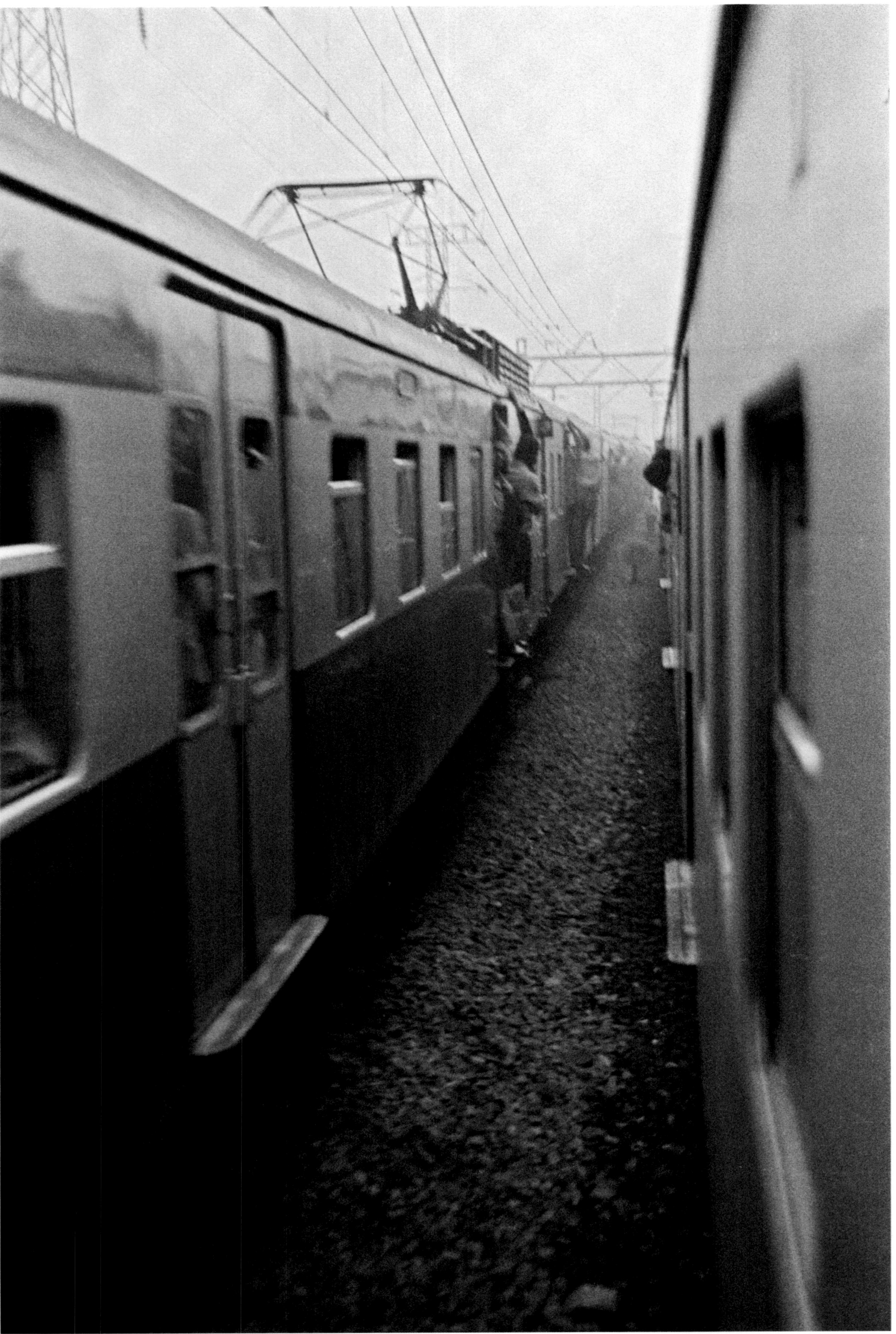

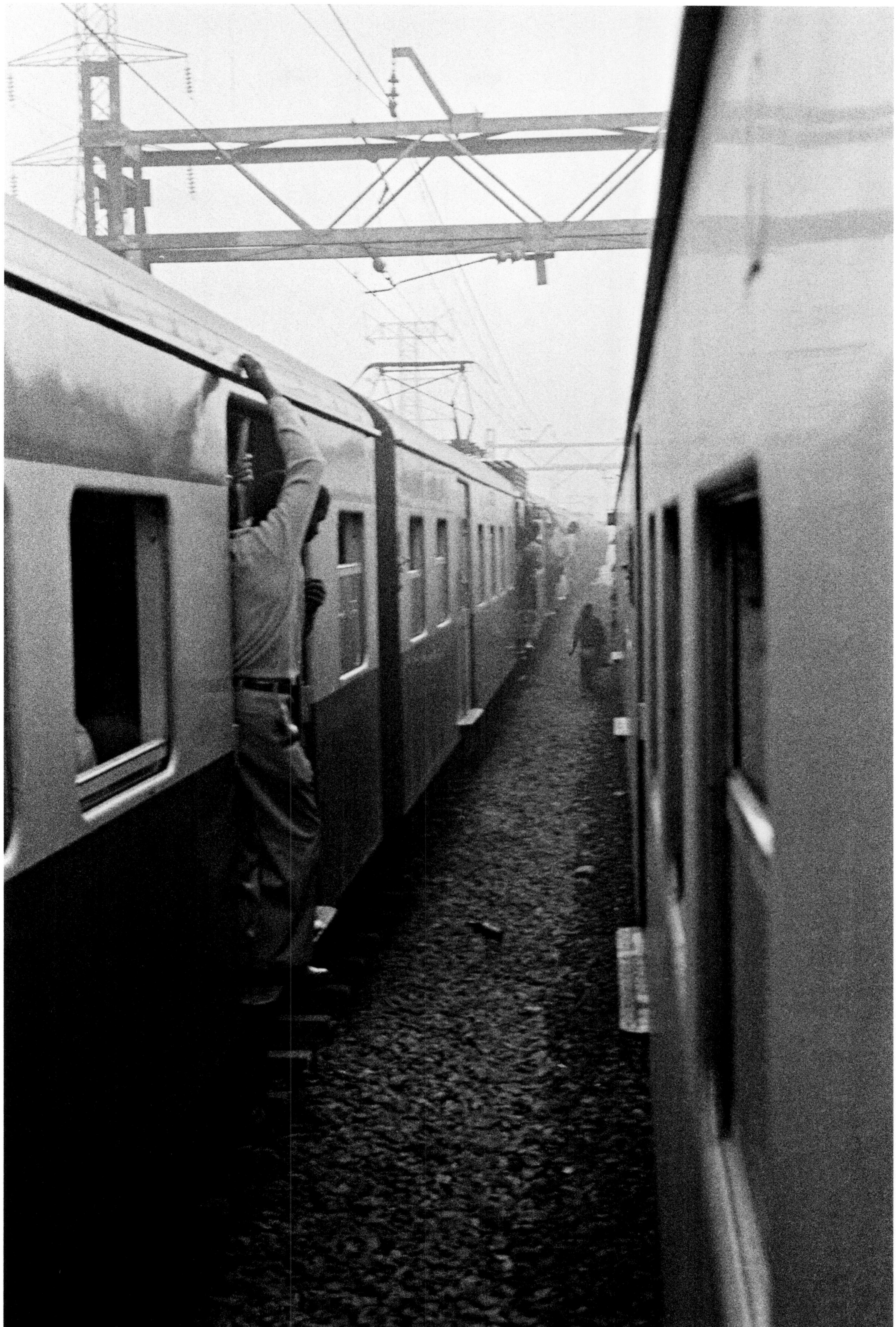

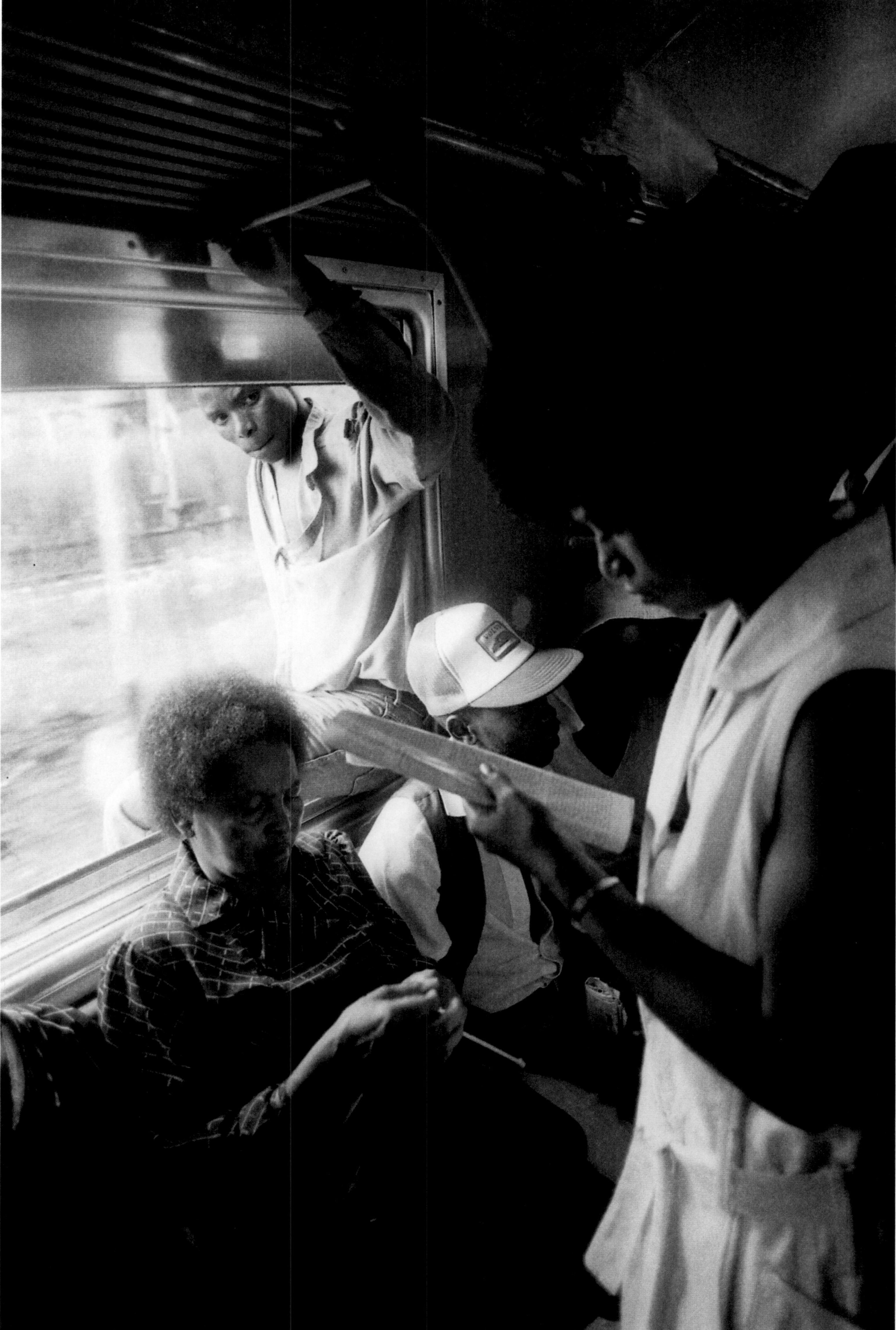

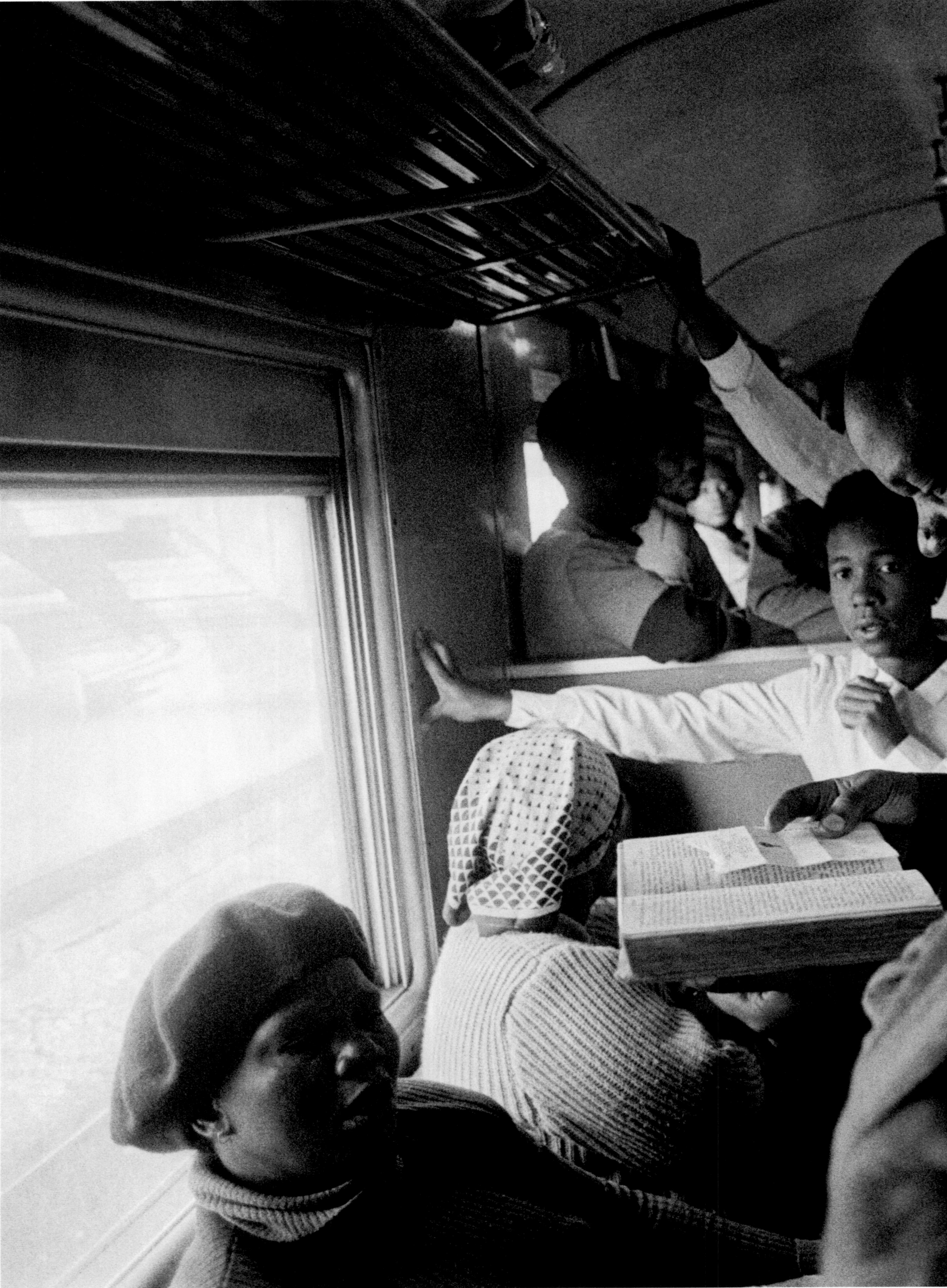

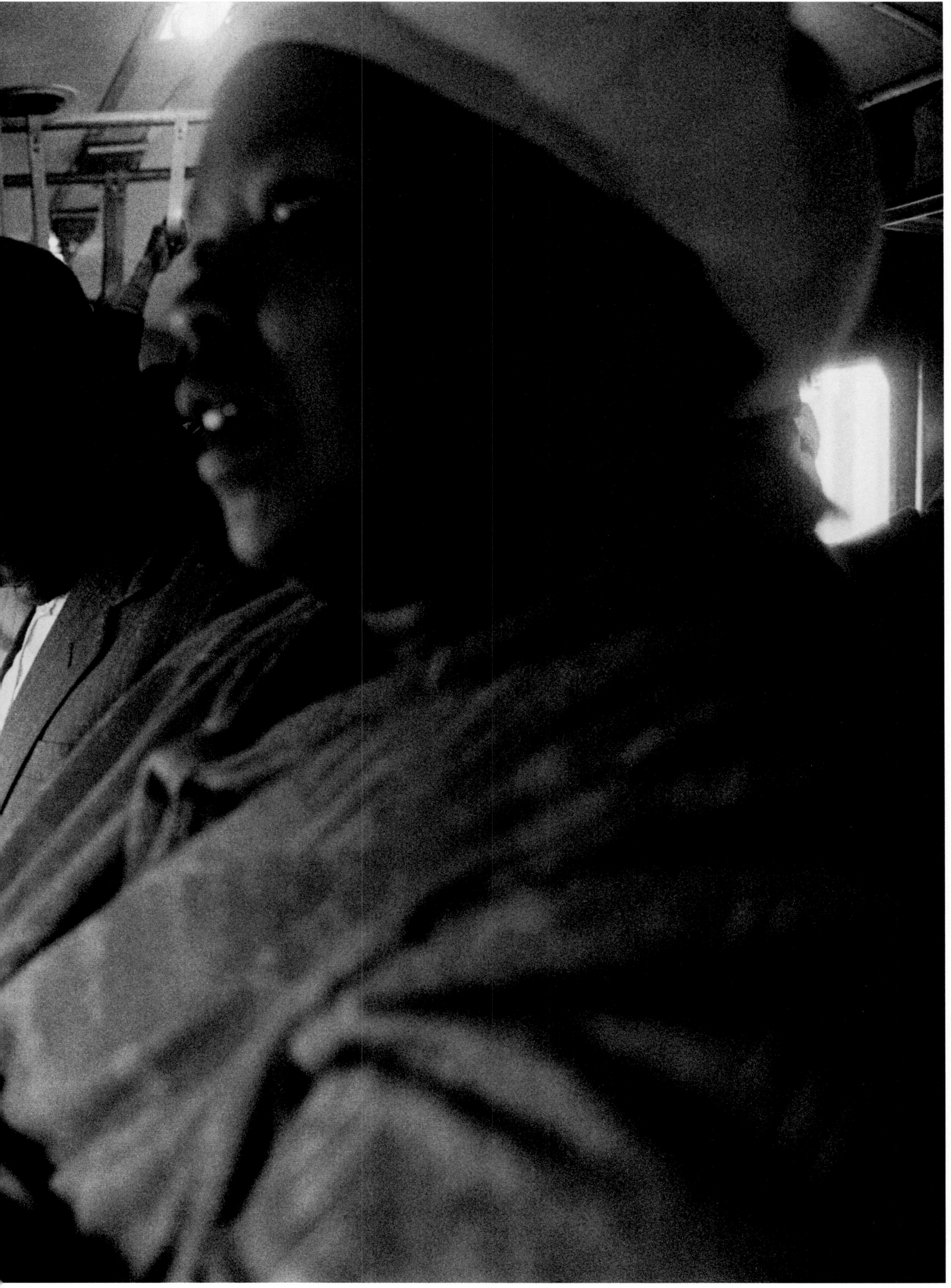

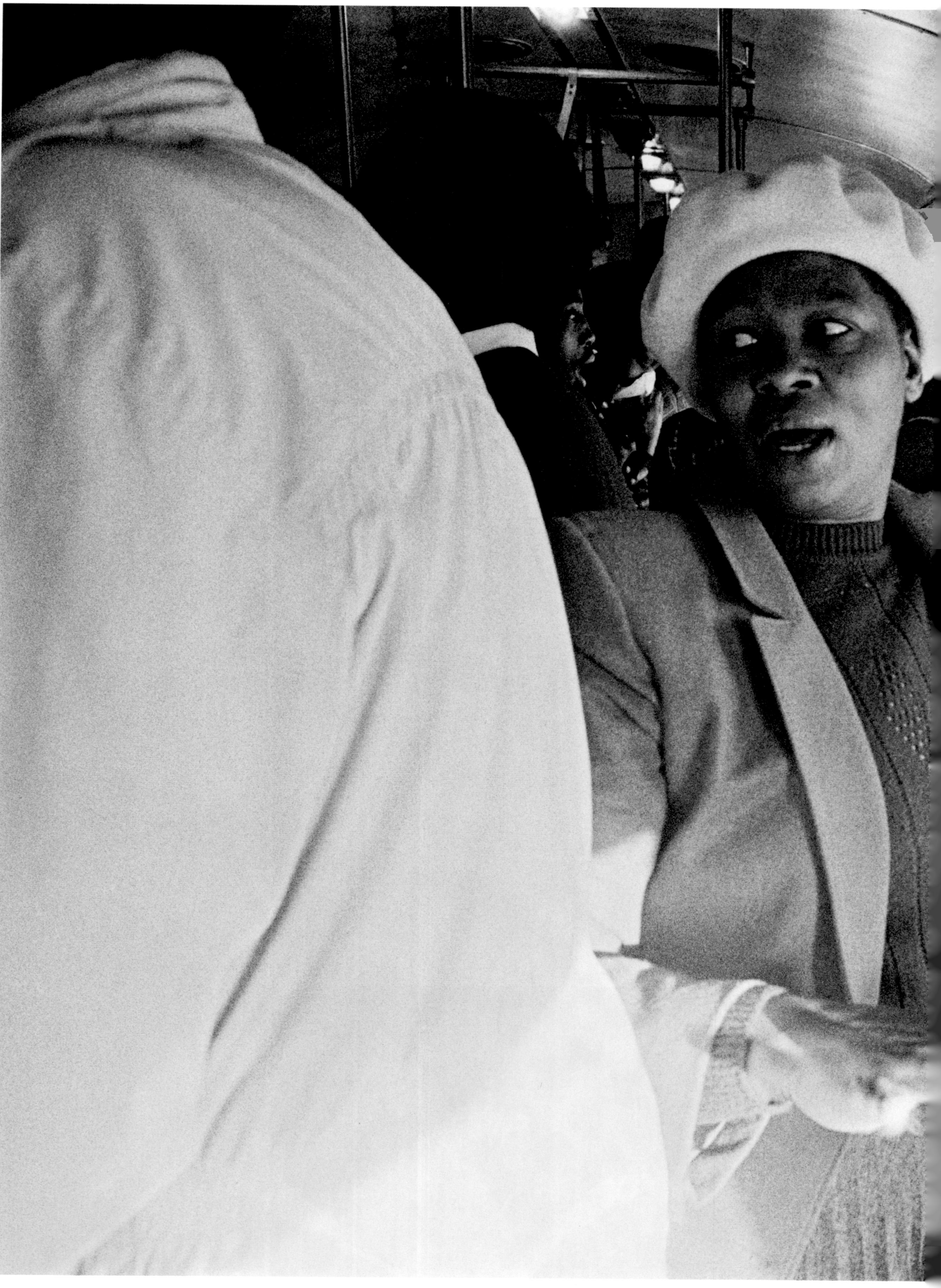

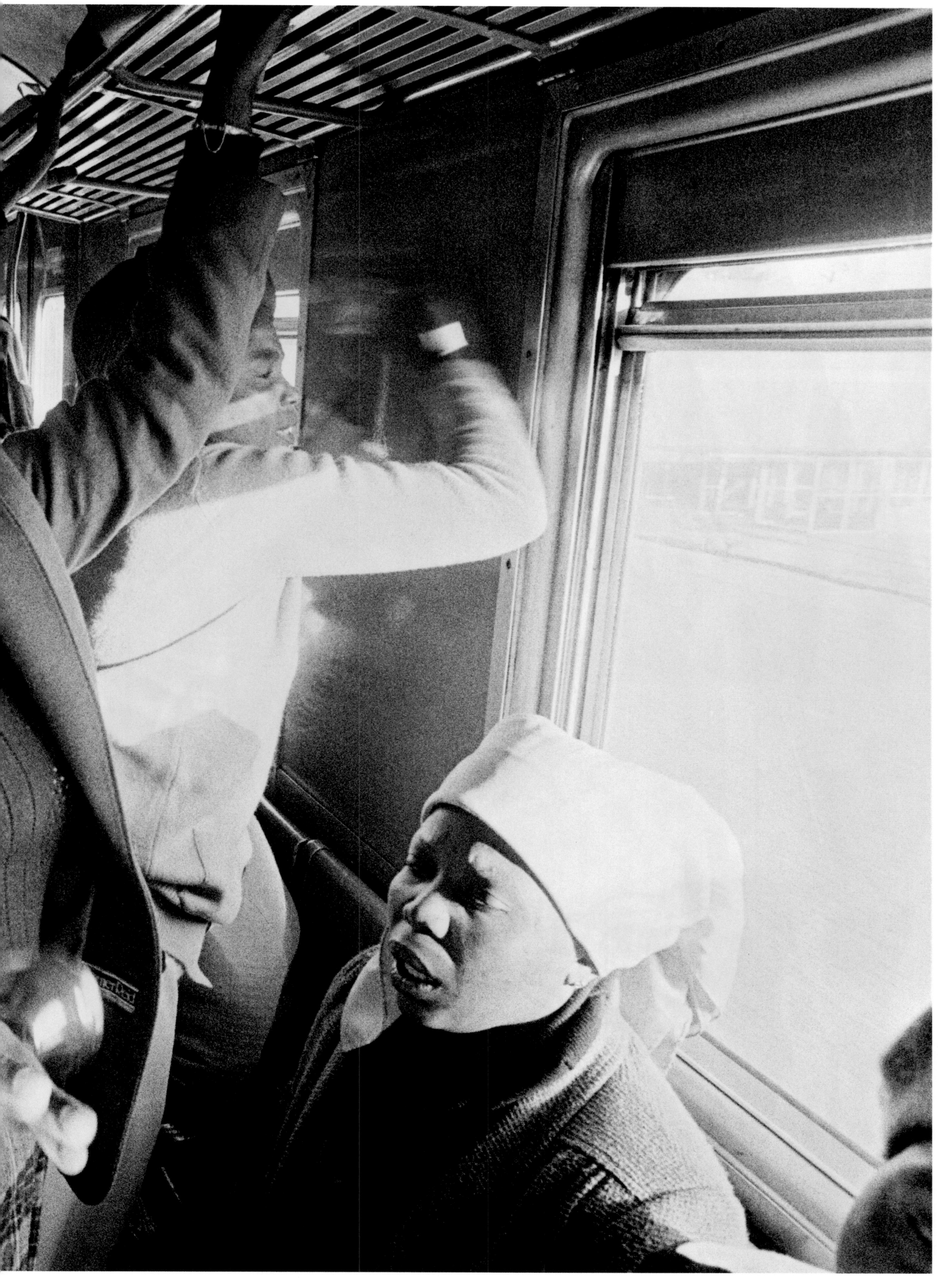

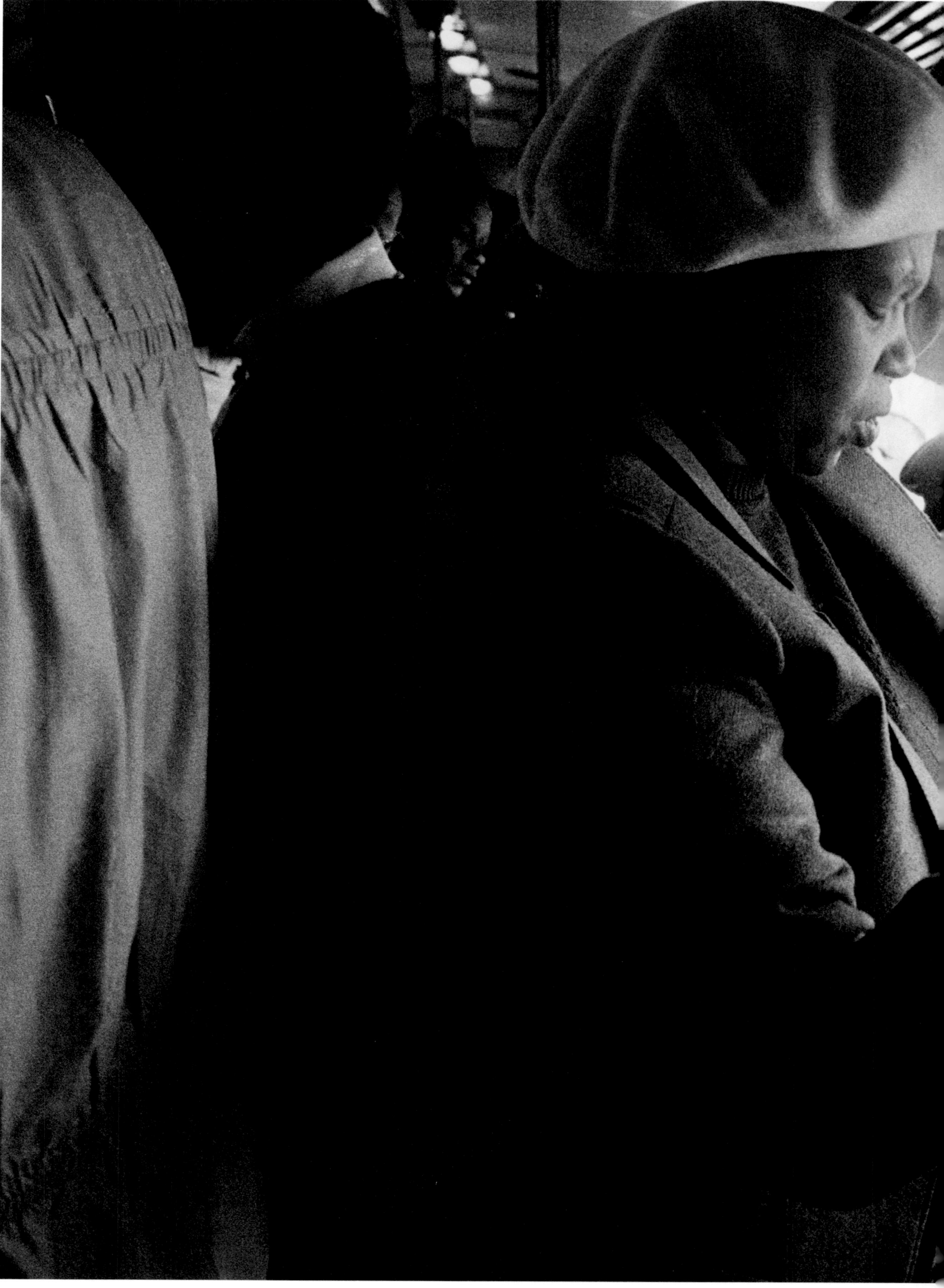

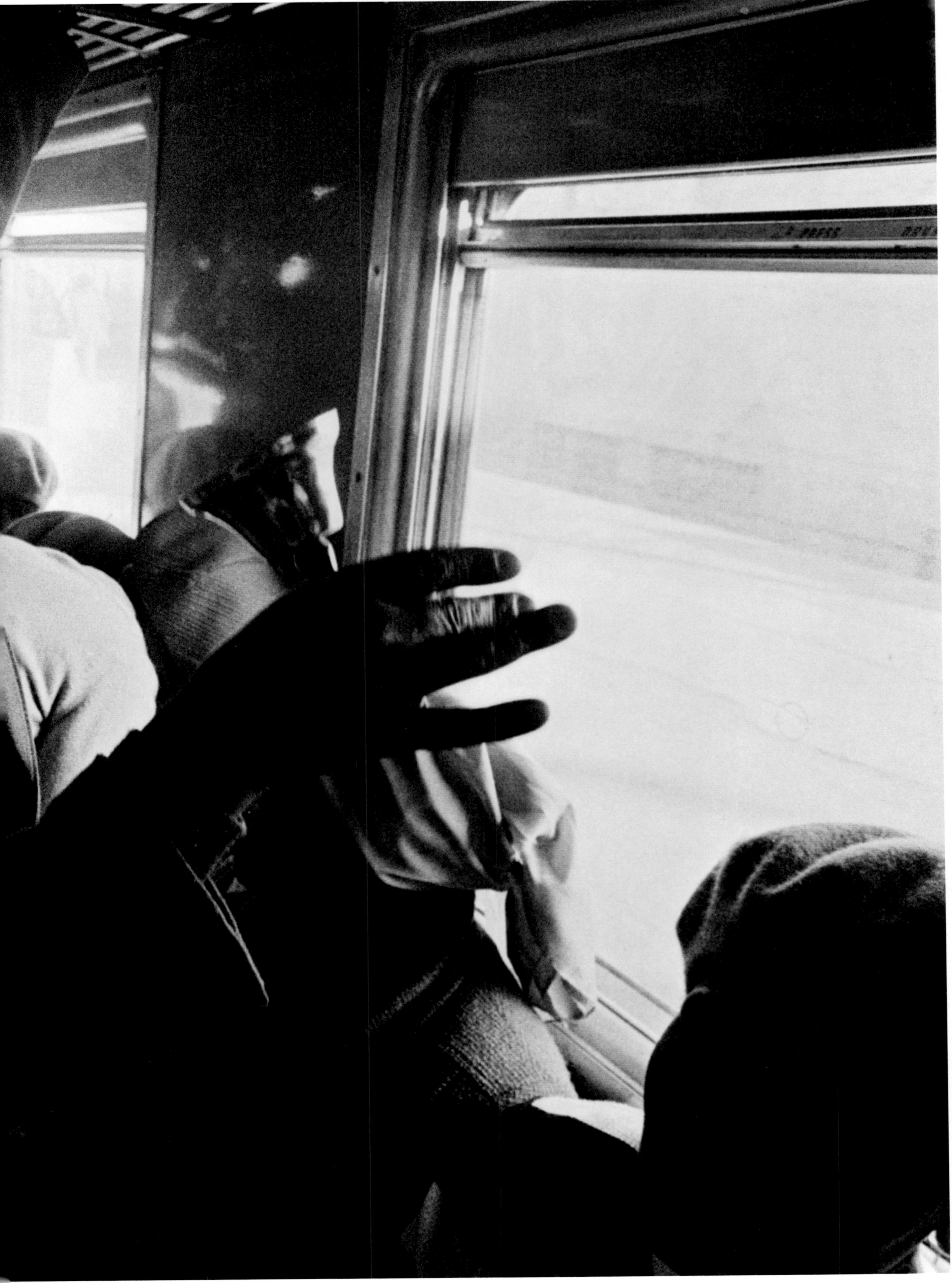

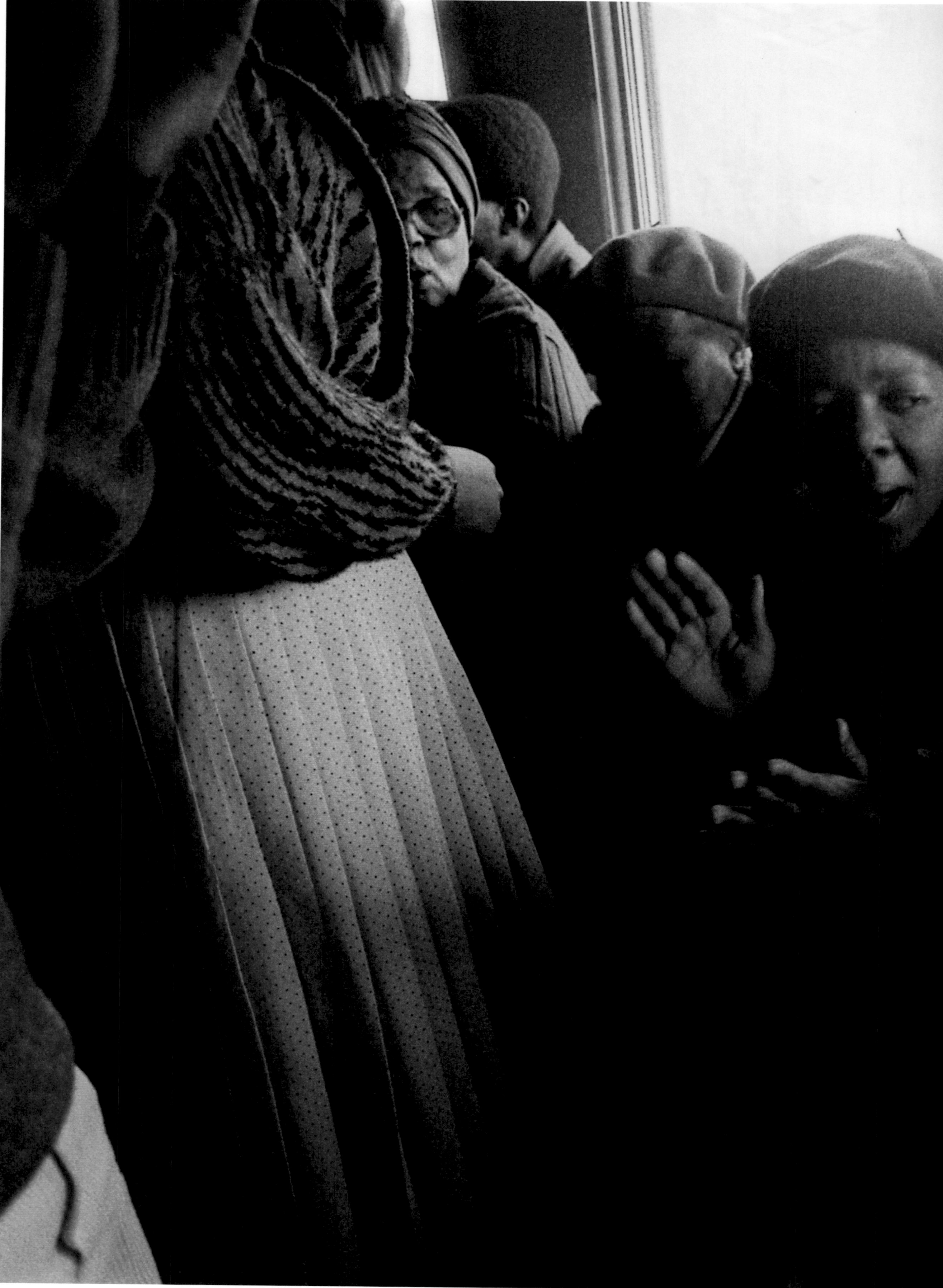

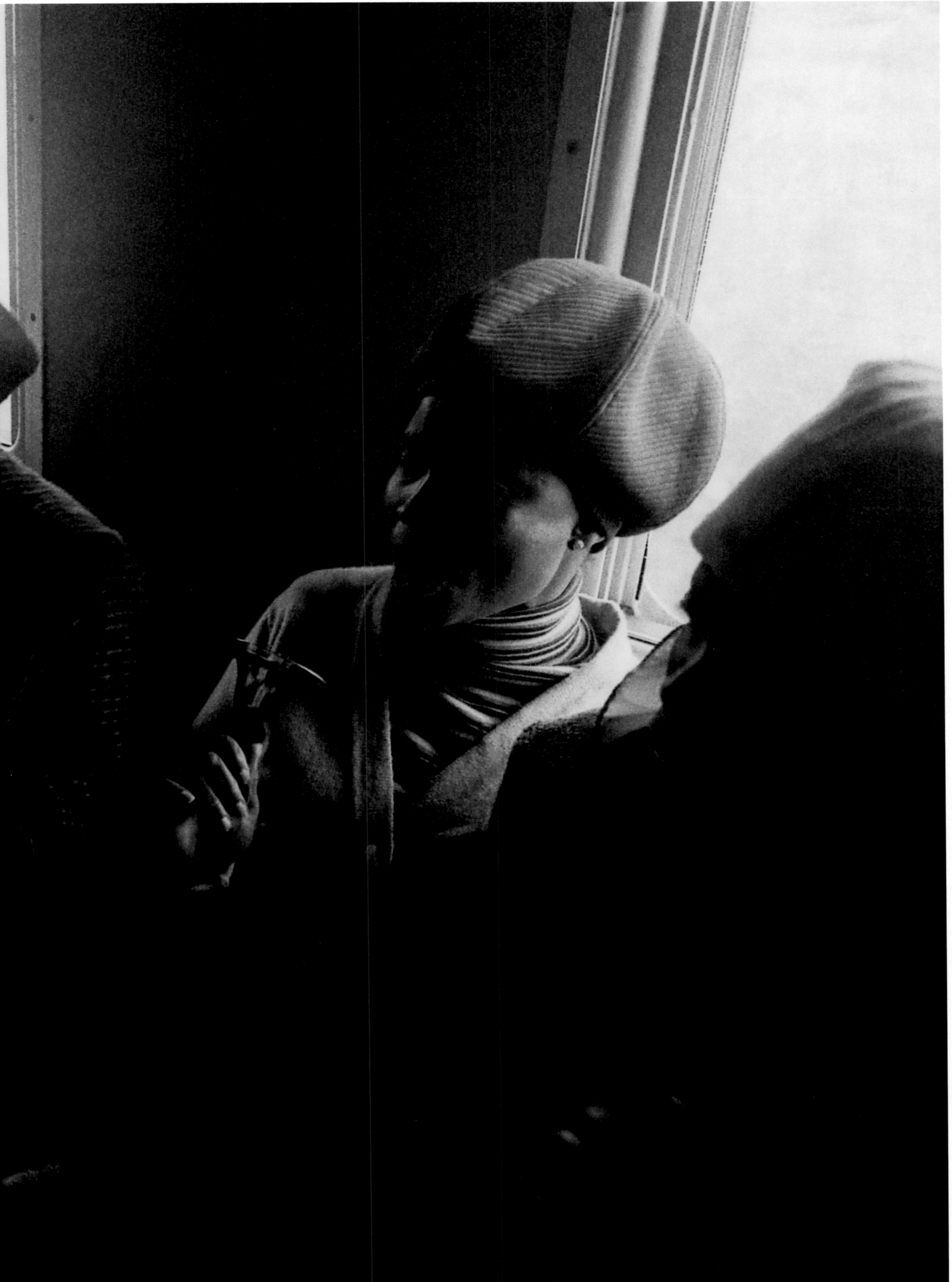

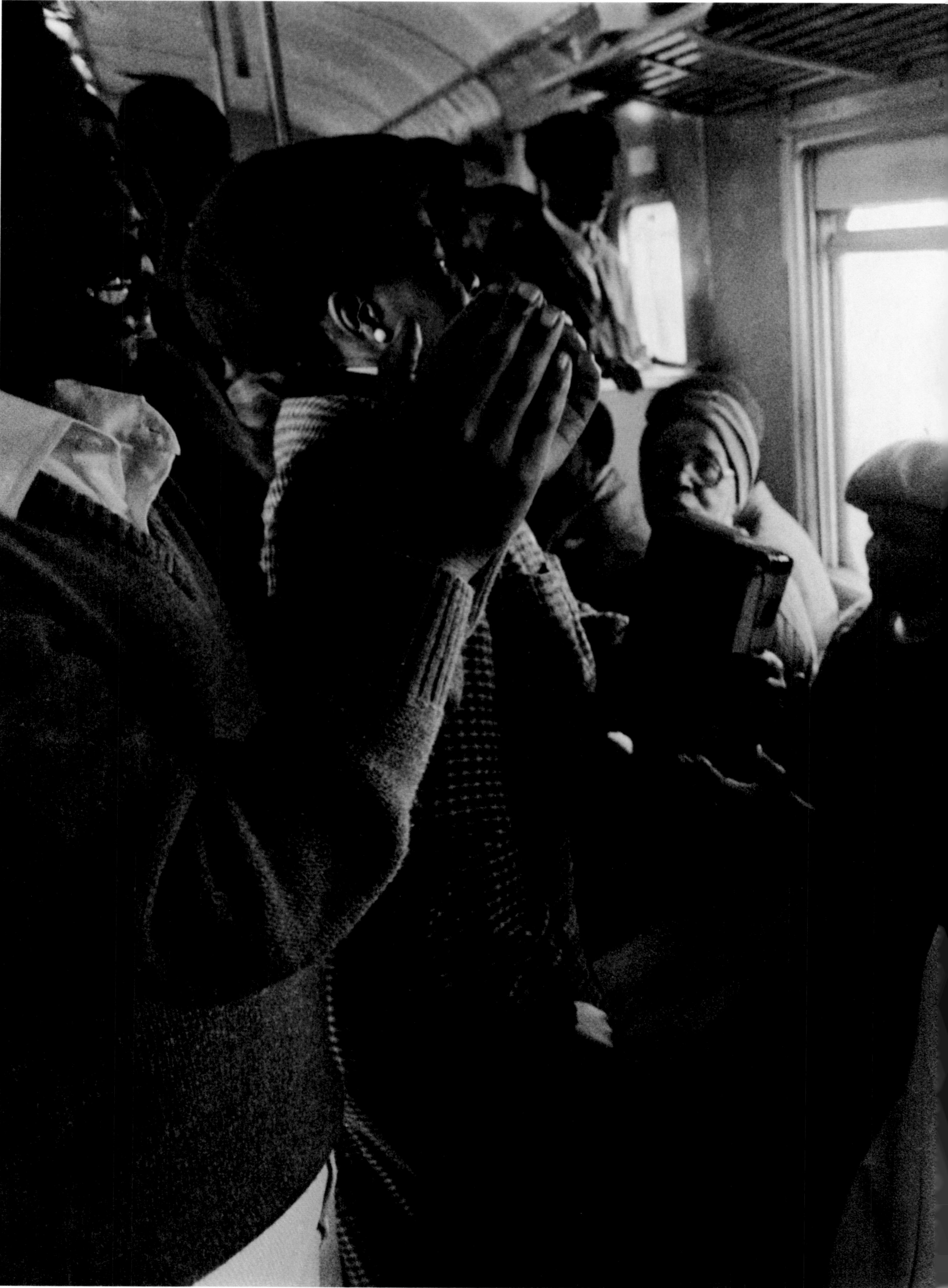

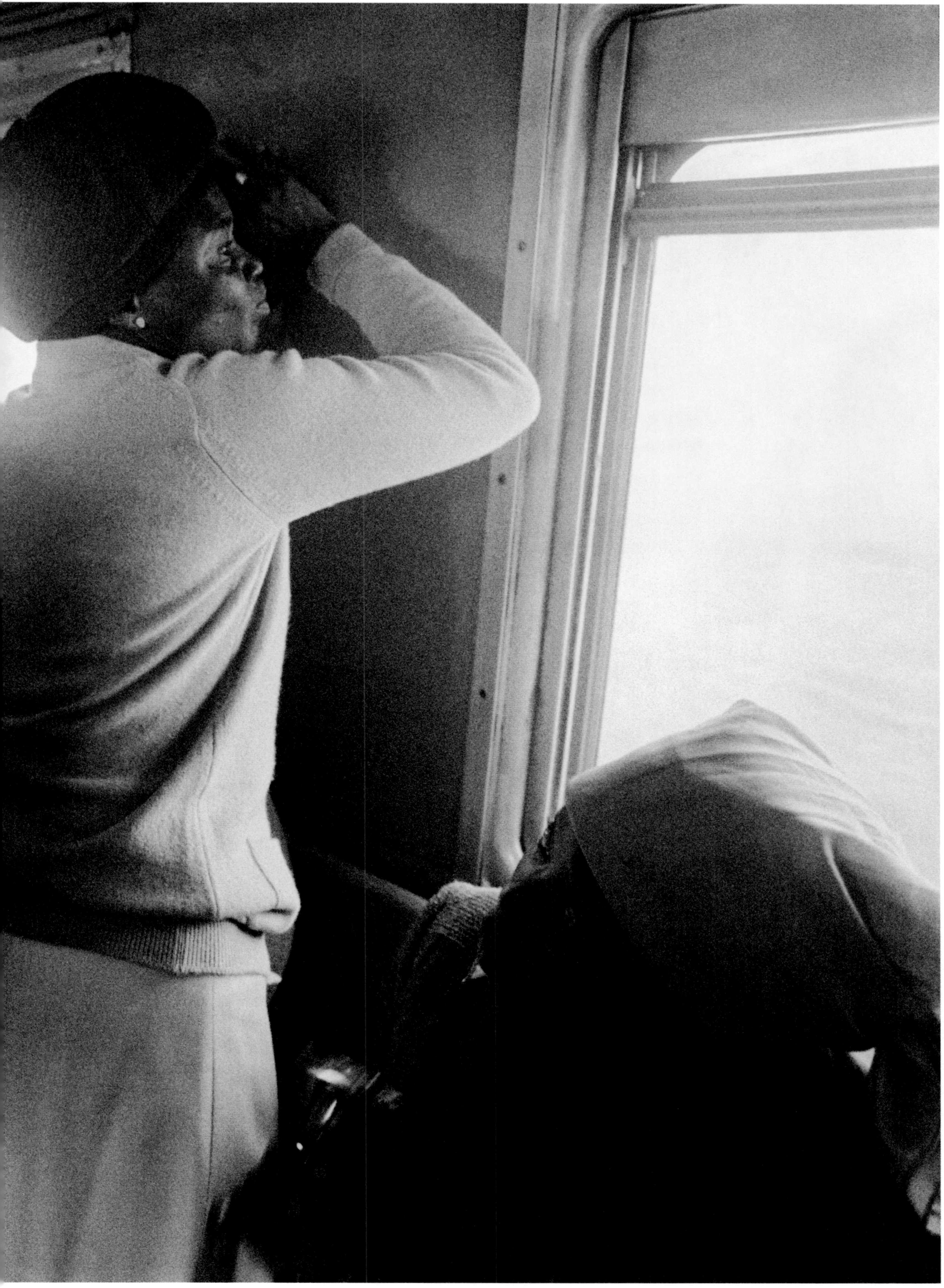

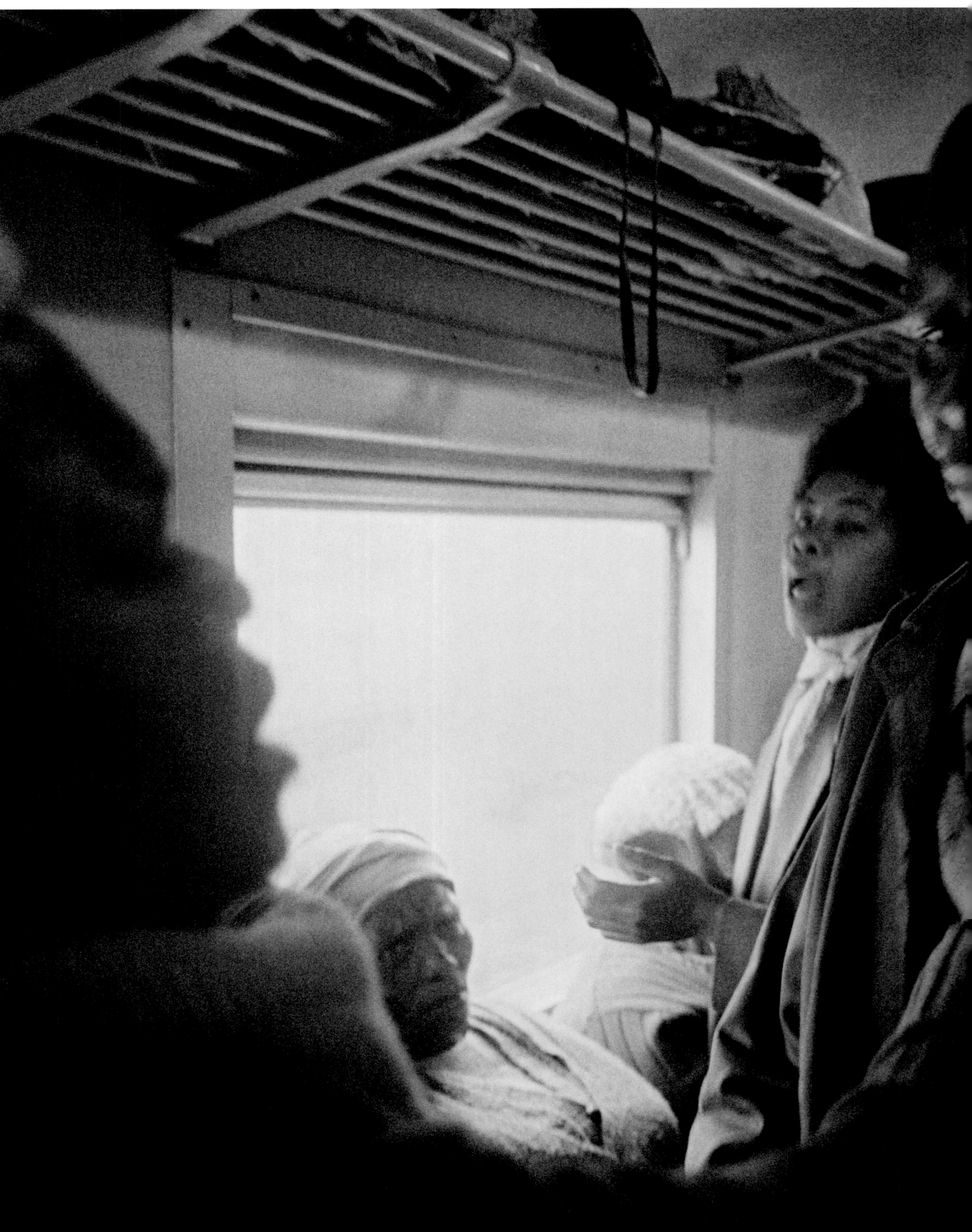

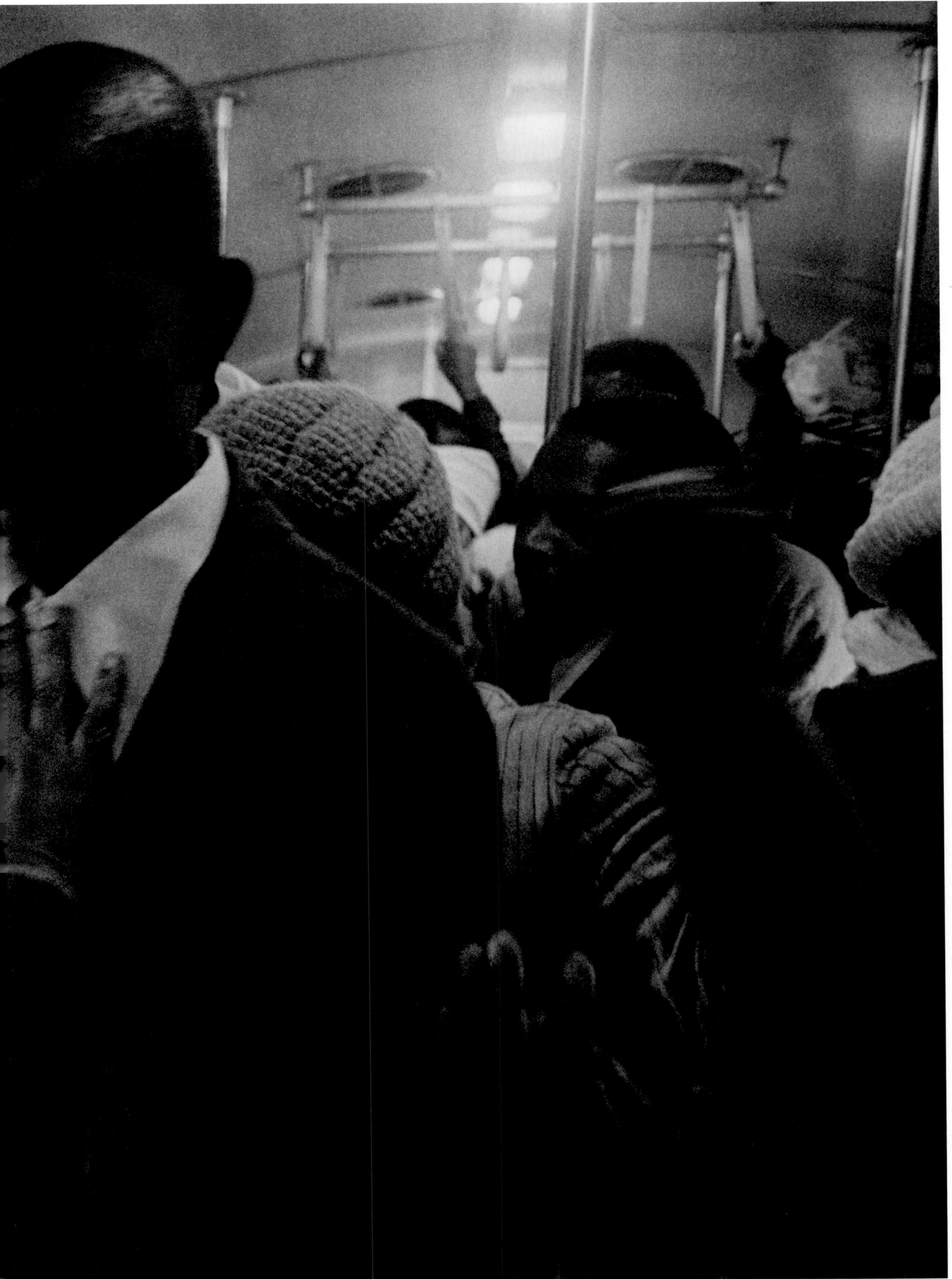

Early-morning, late-afternoon and evening commuters preach the gospel in trains en route to and from work.

The train ride is no longer a means to an end, but an end in itself as people from different townships congregate in coaches – two or three per train – to sing to the accompaniment of improvised drums (banging the sides of the train) and bells.

Foot stomping and gyrating – a packed train is turned into a church.

This is a daily ritual.

This sudden religious ecstasy struck me as odd. These office cleaners, clerks, factory workers and general labourers enjoined in a cacophony of song and prayer, a catharsis of spirituality in a moving landscape.

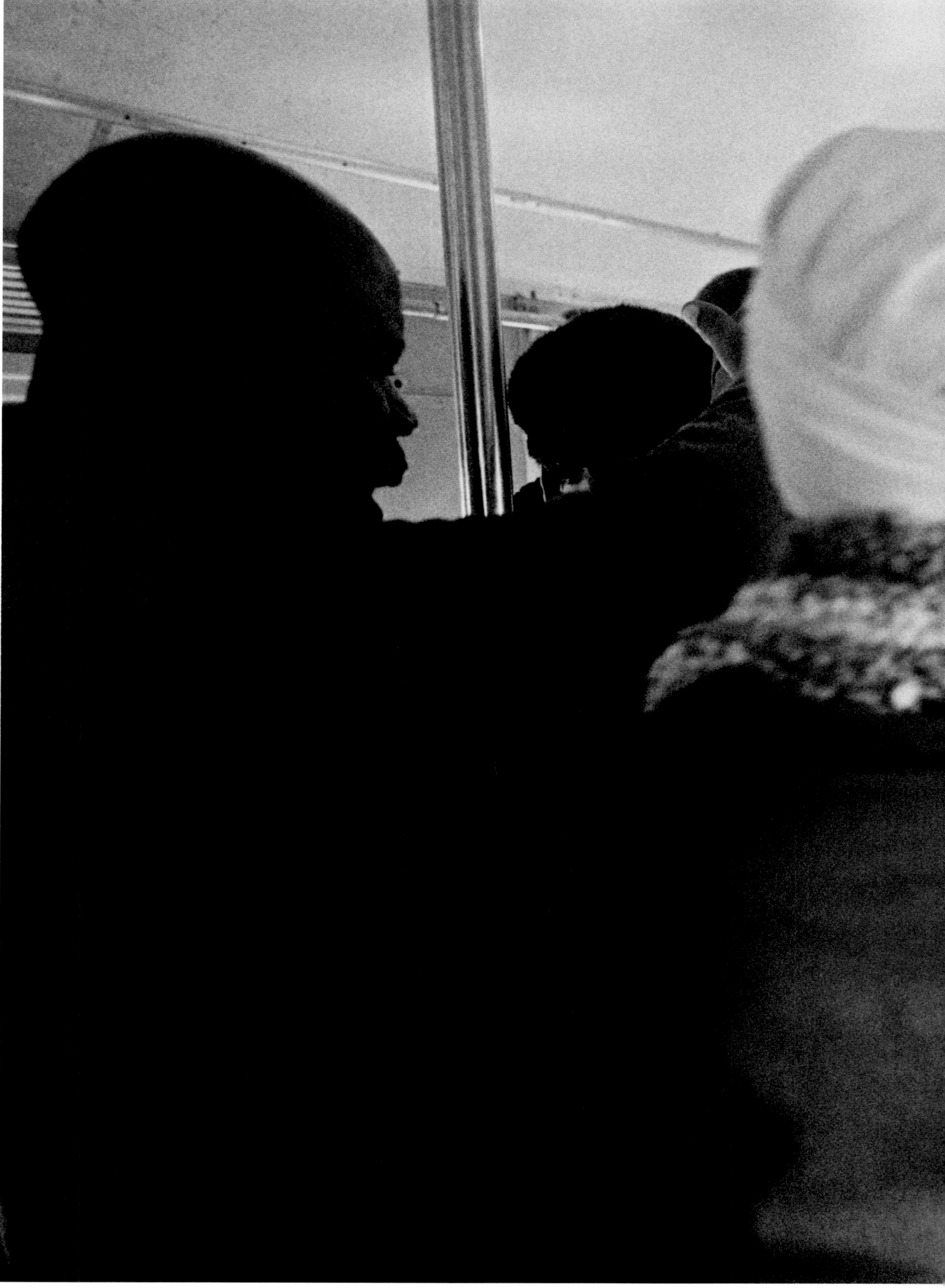

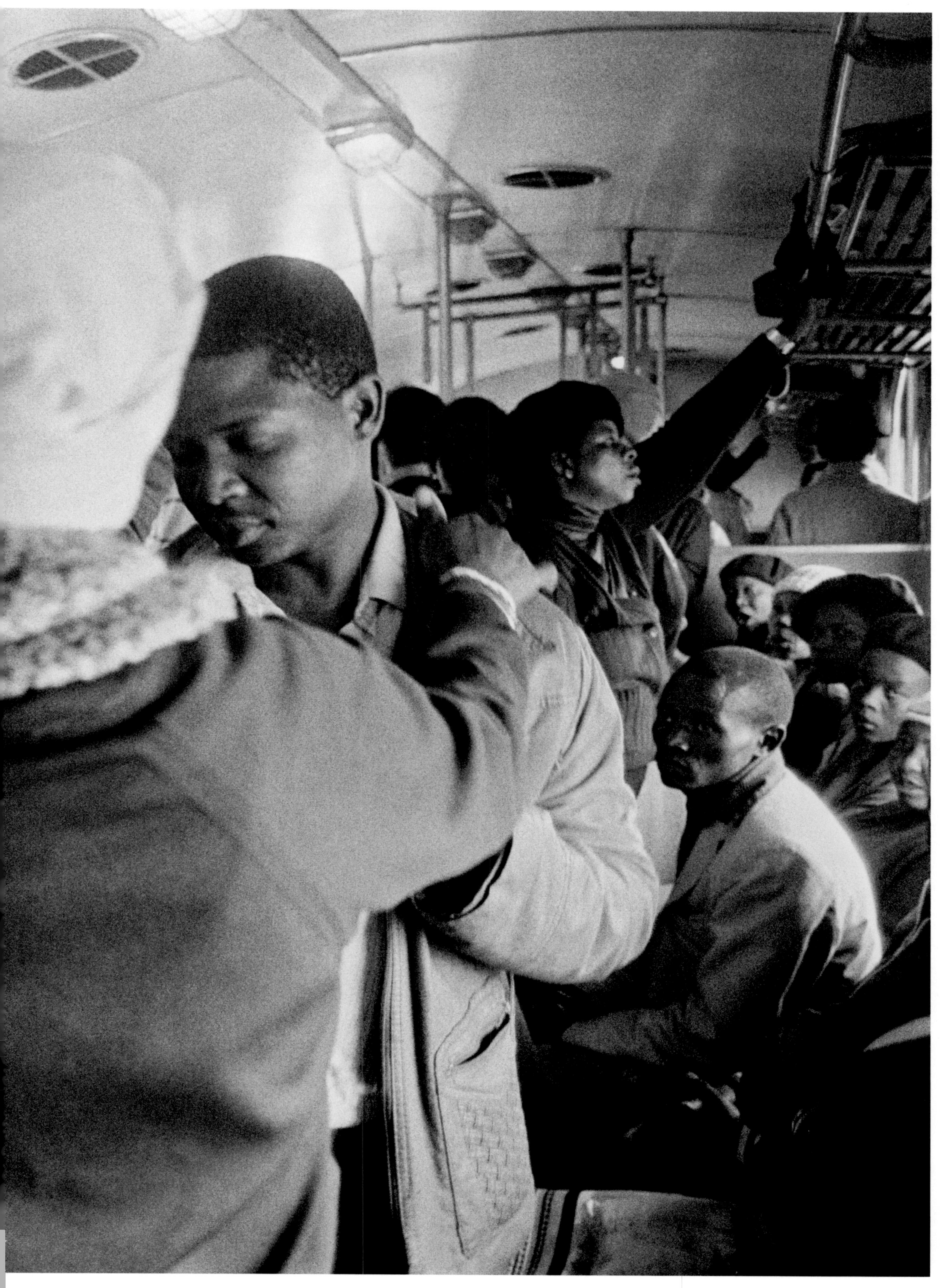

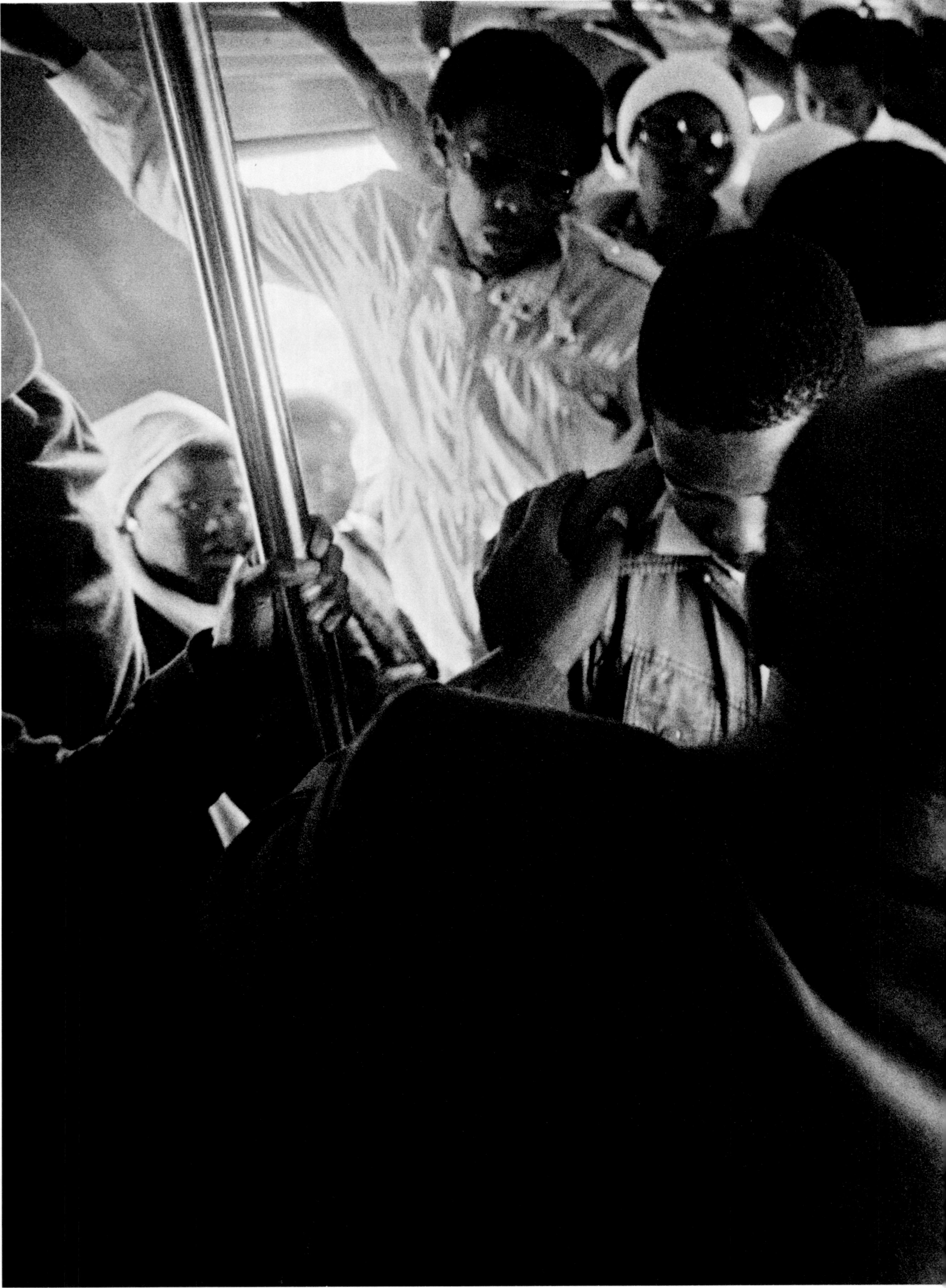

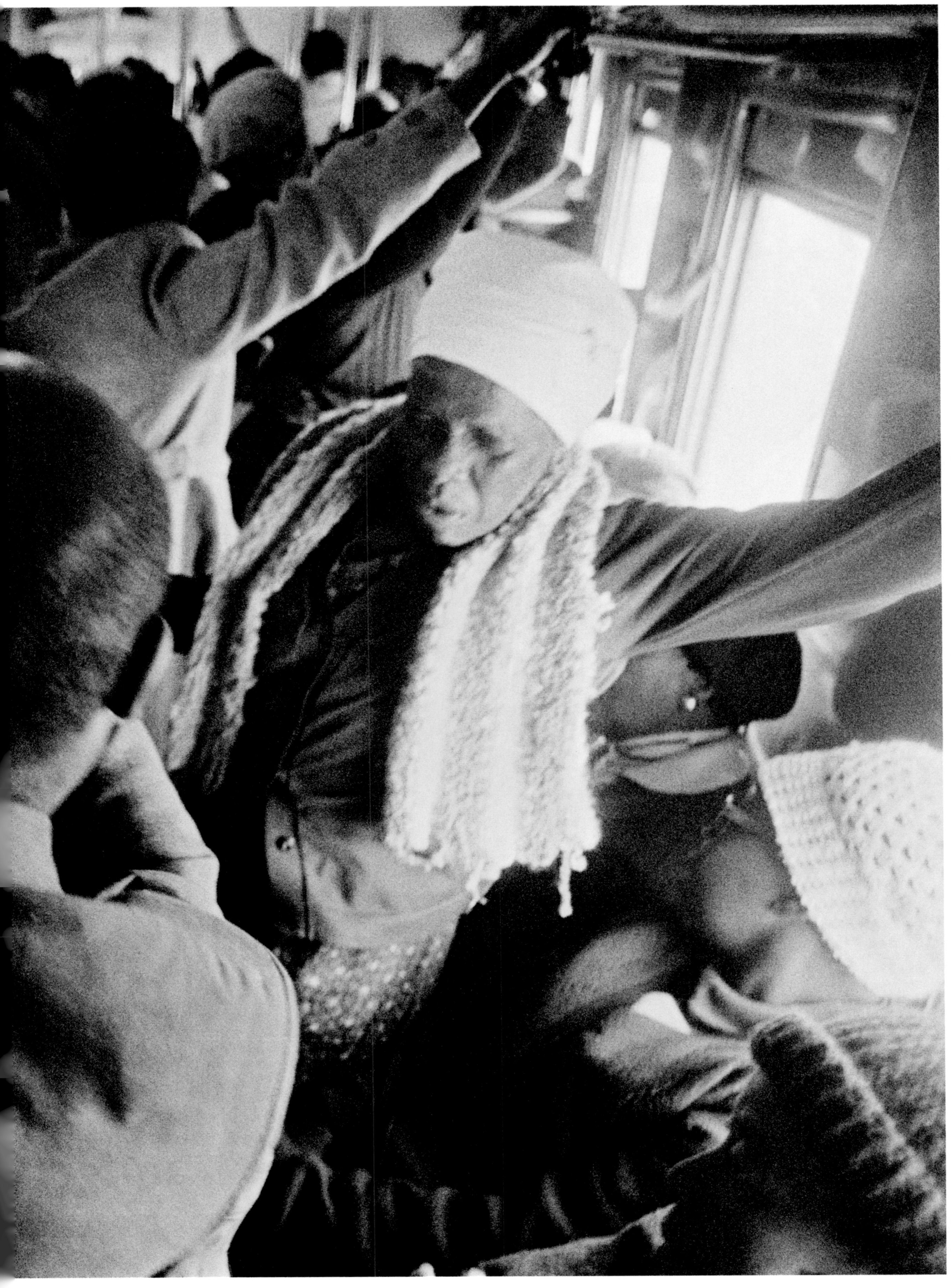

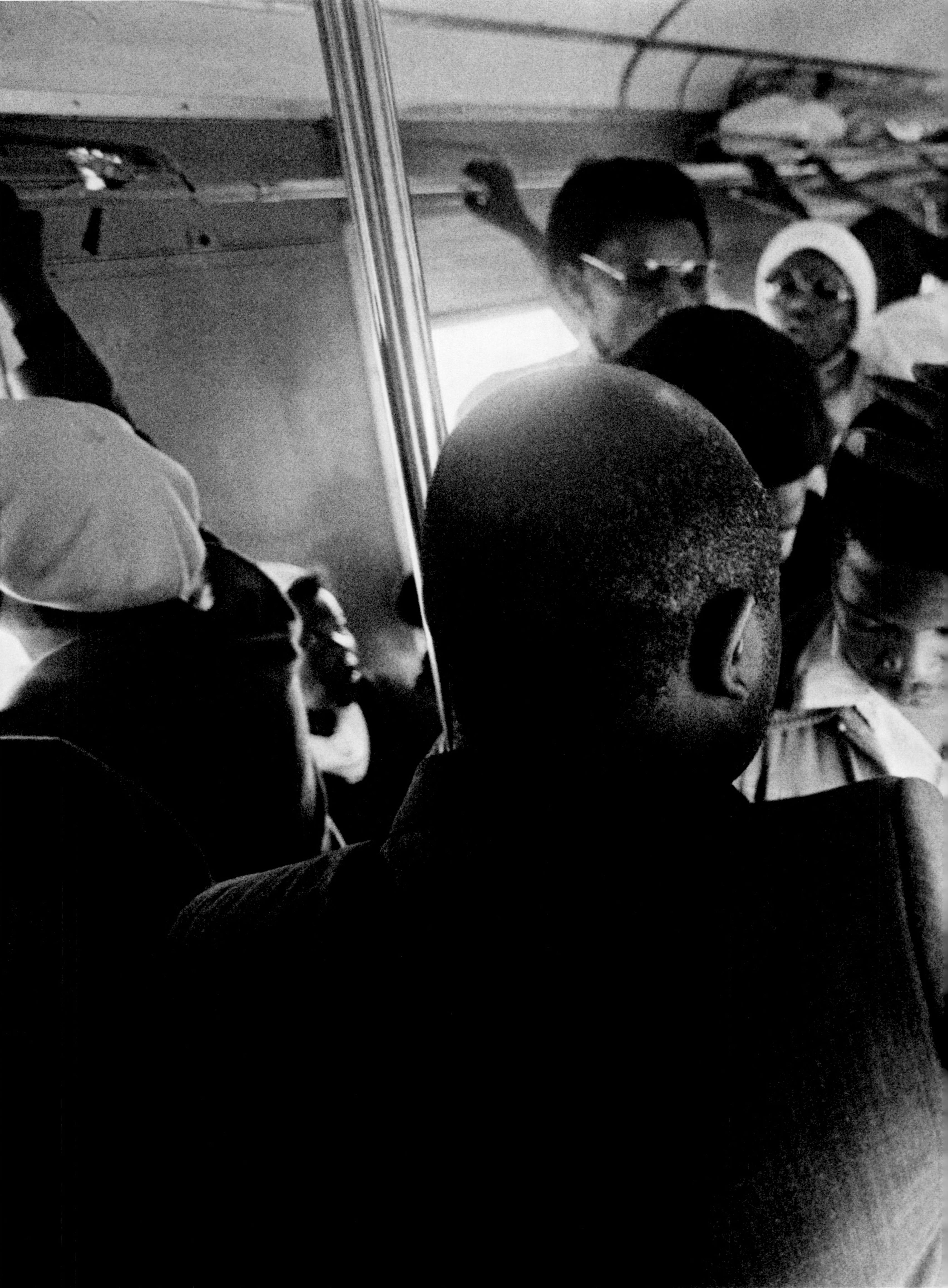

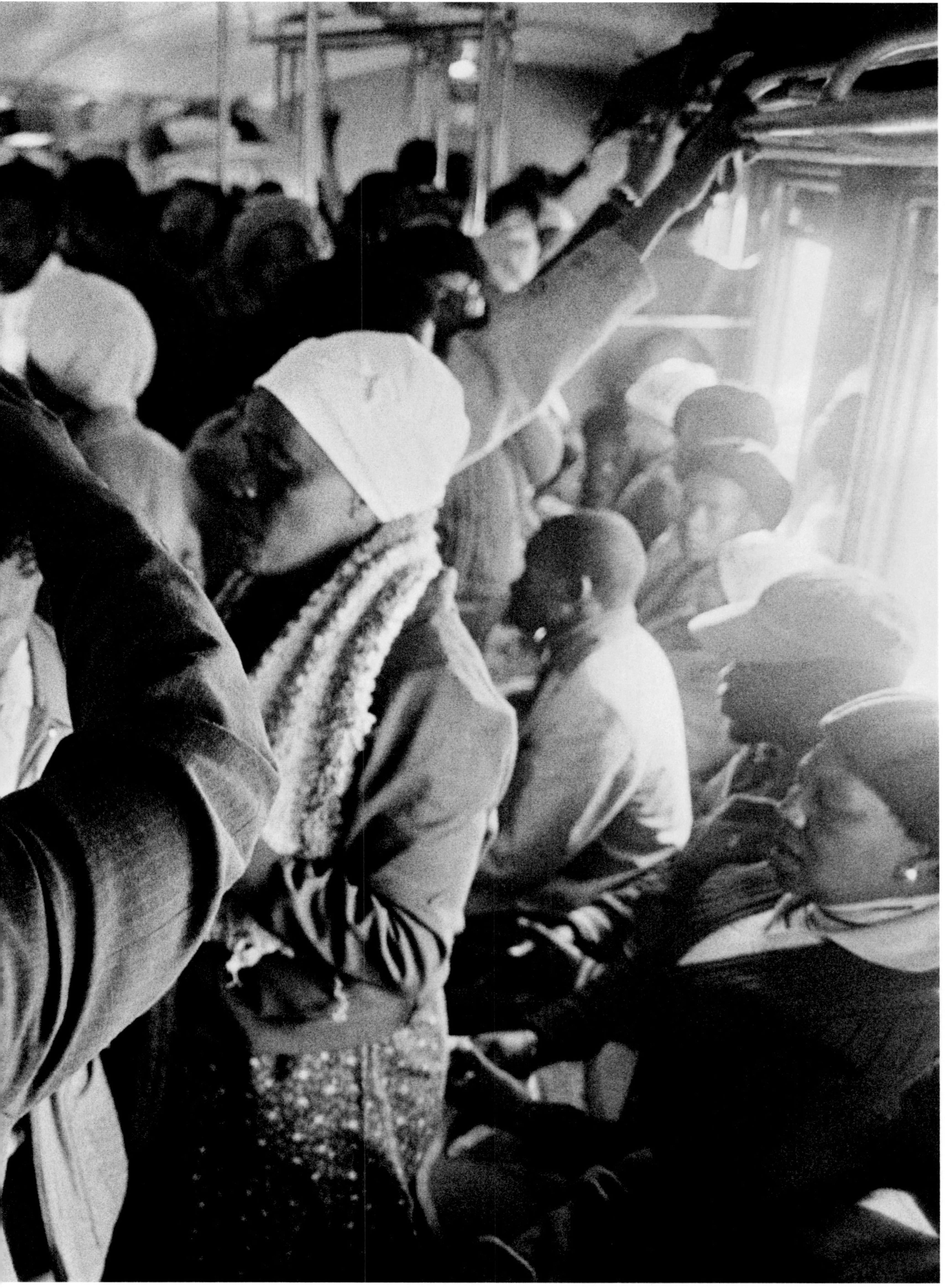

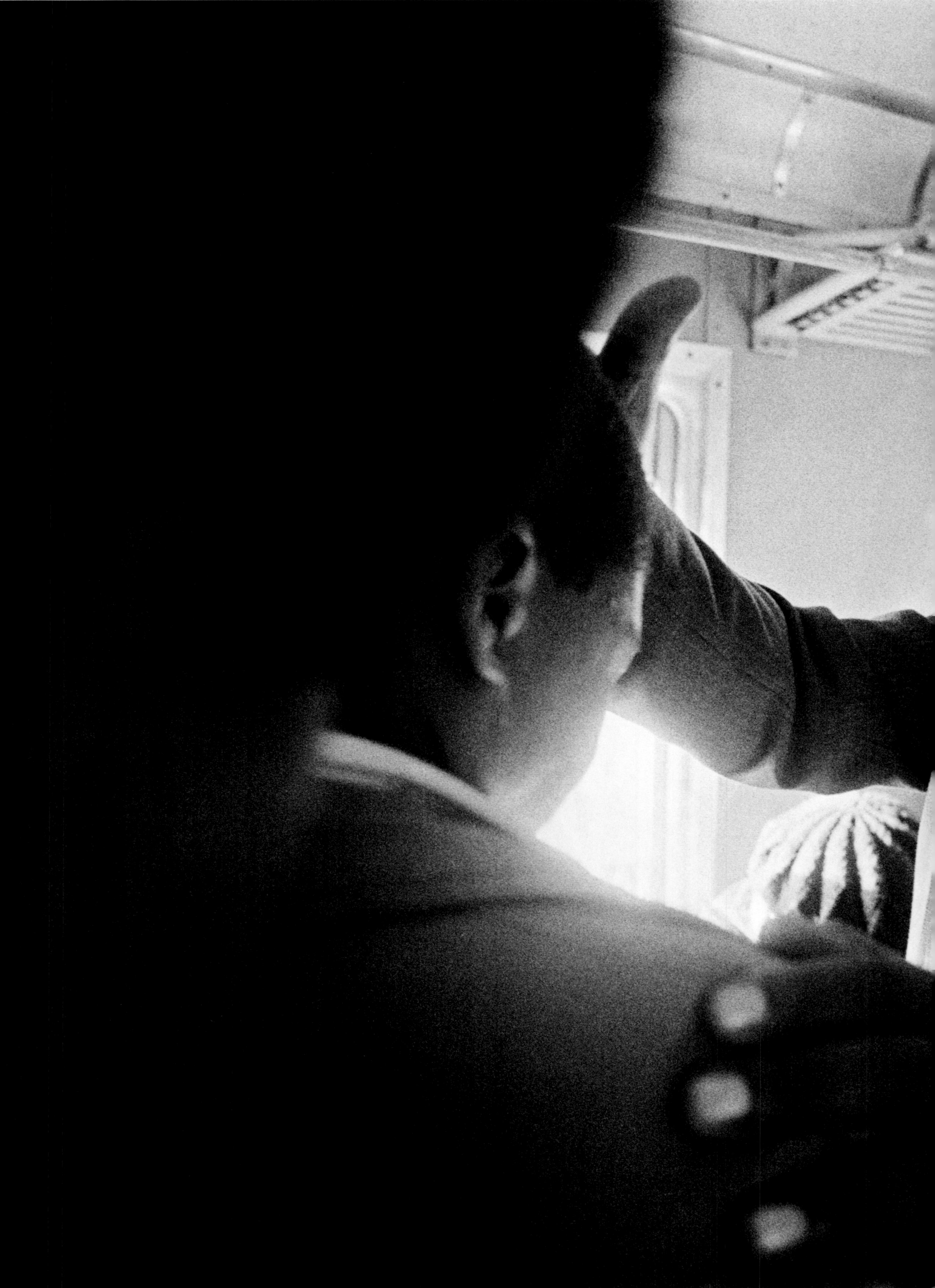

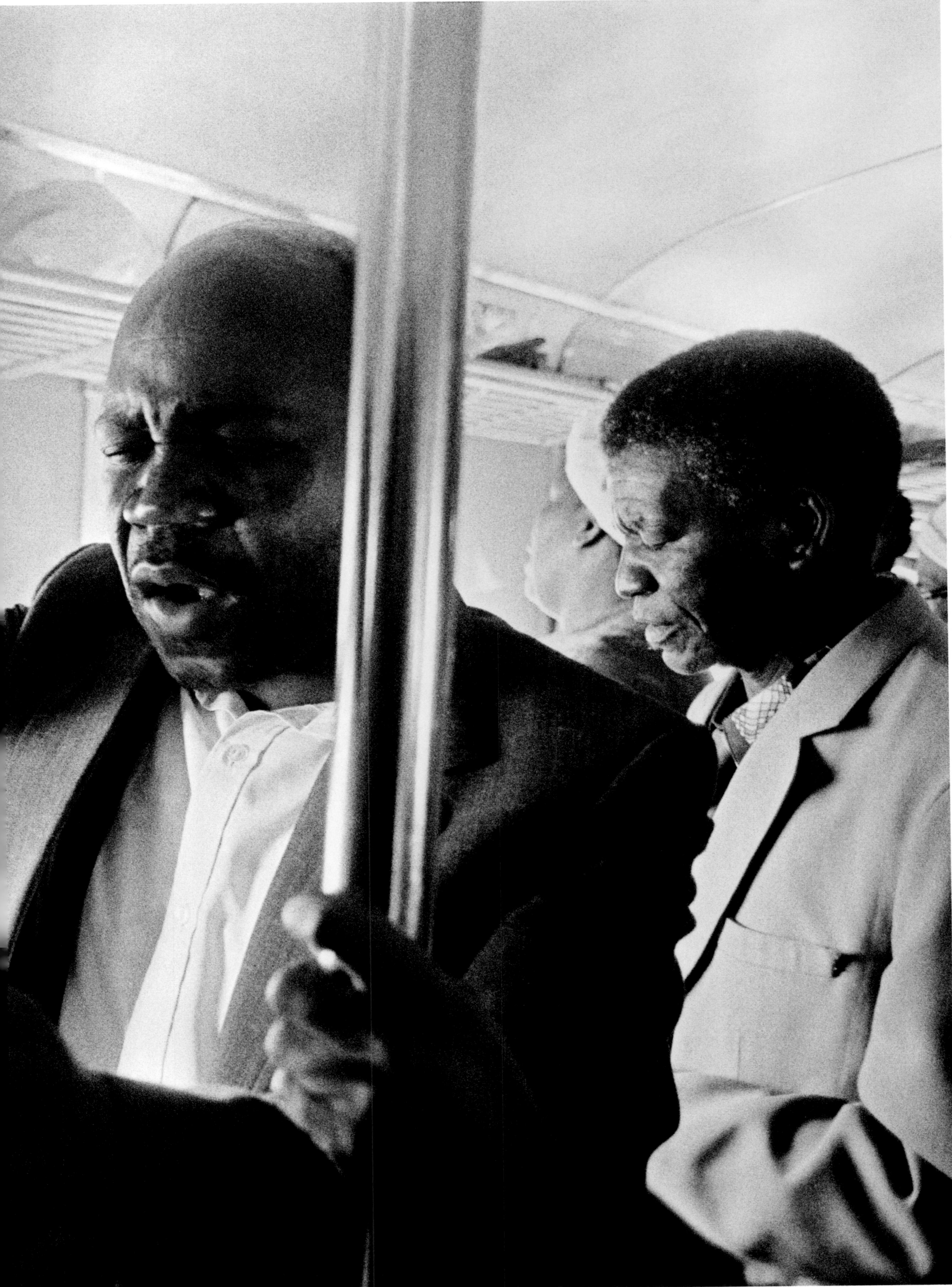

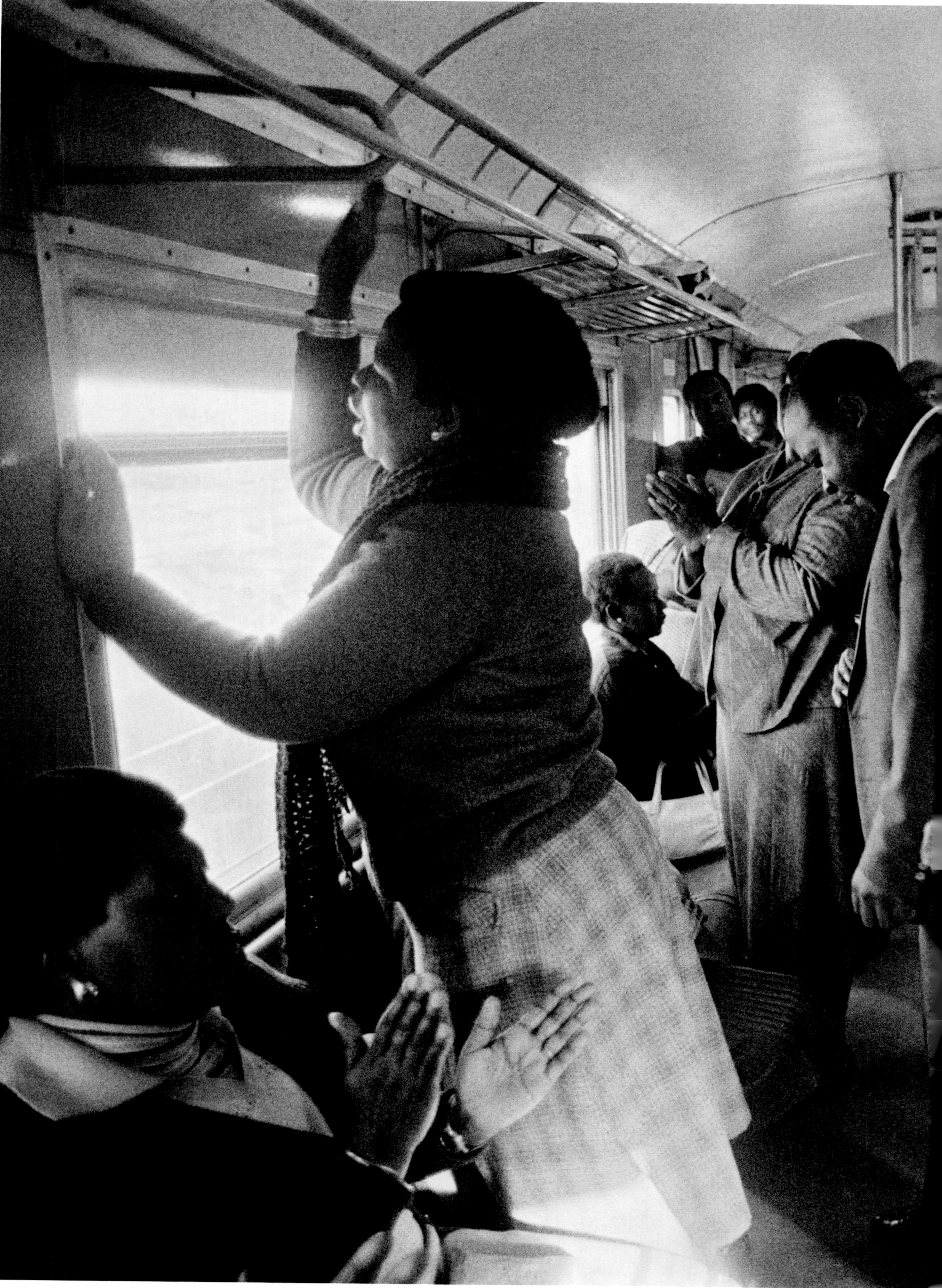

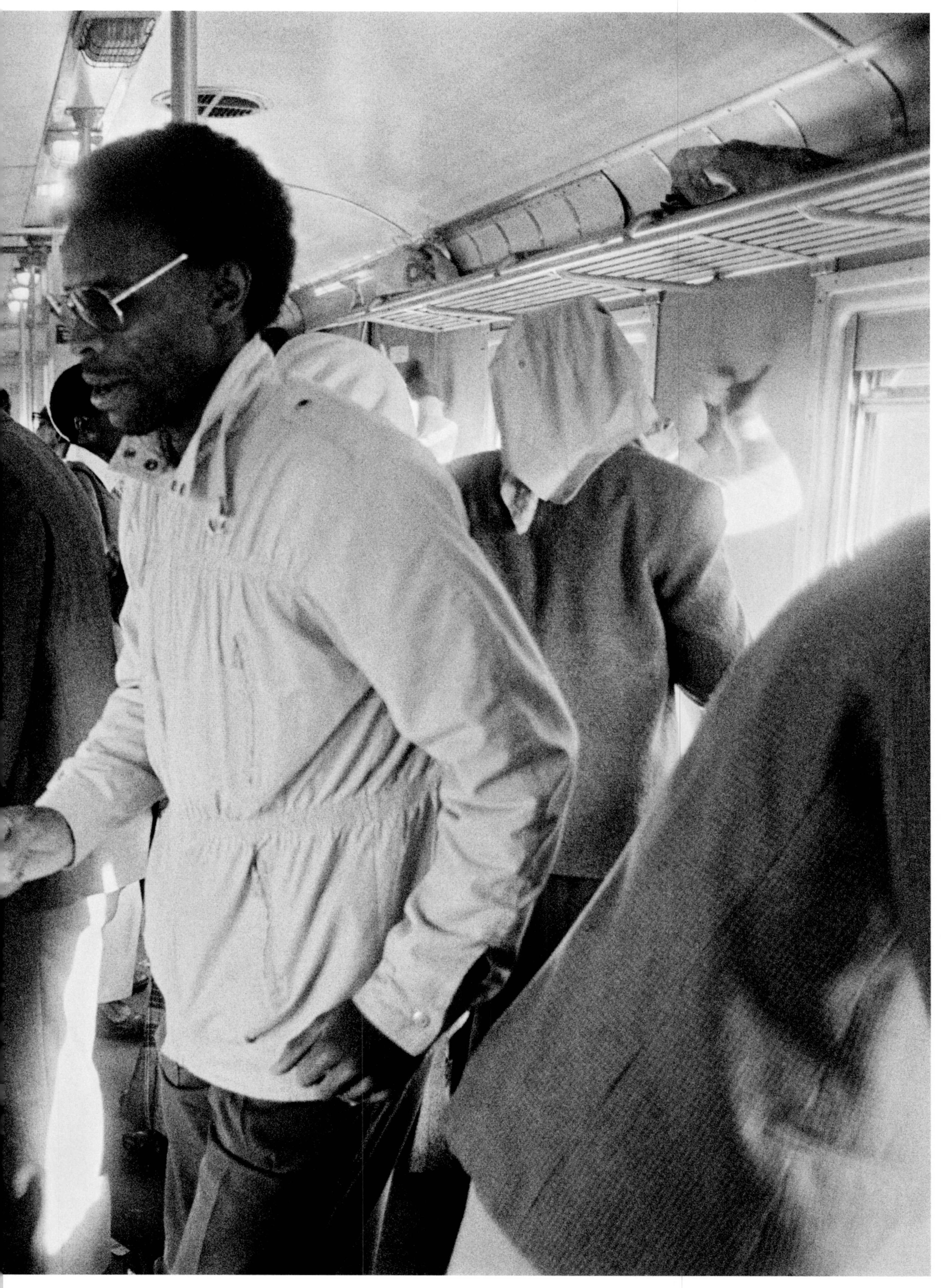

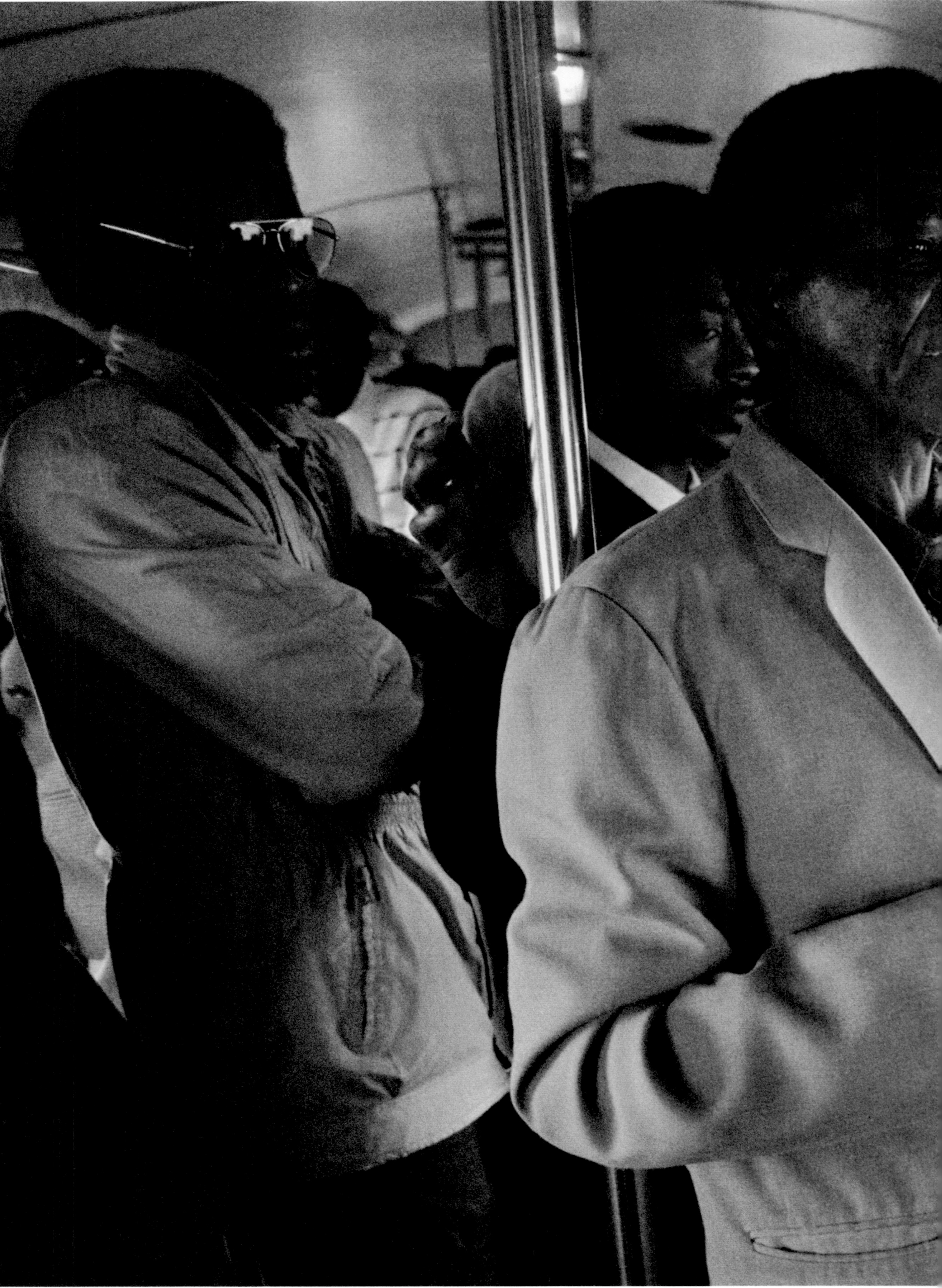

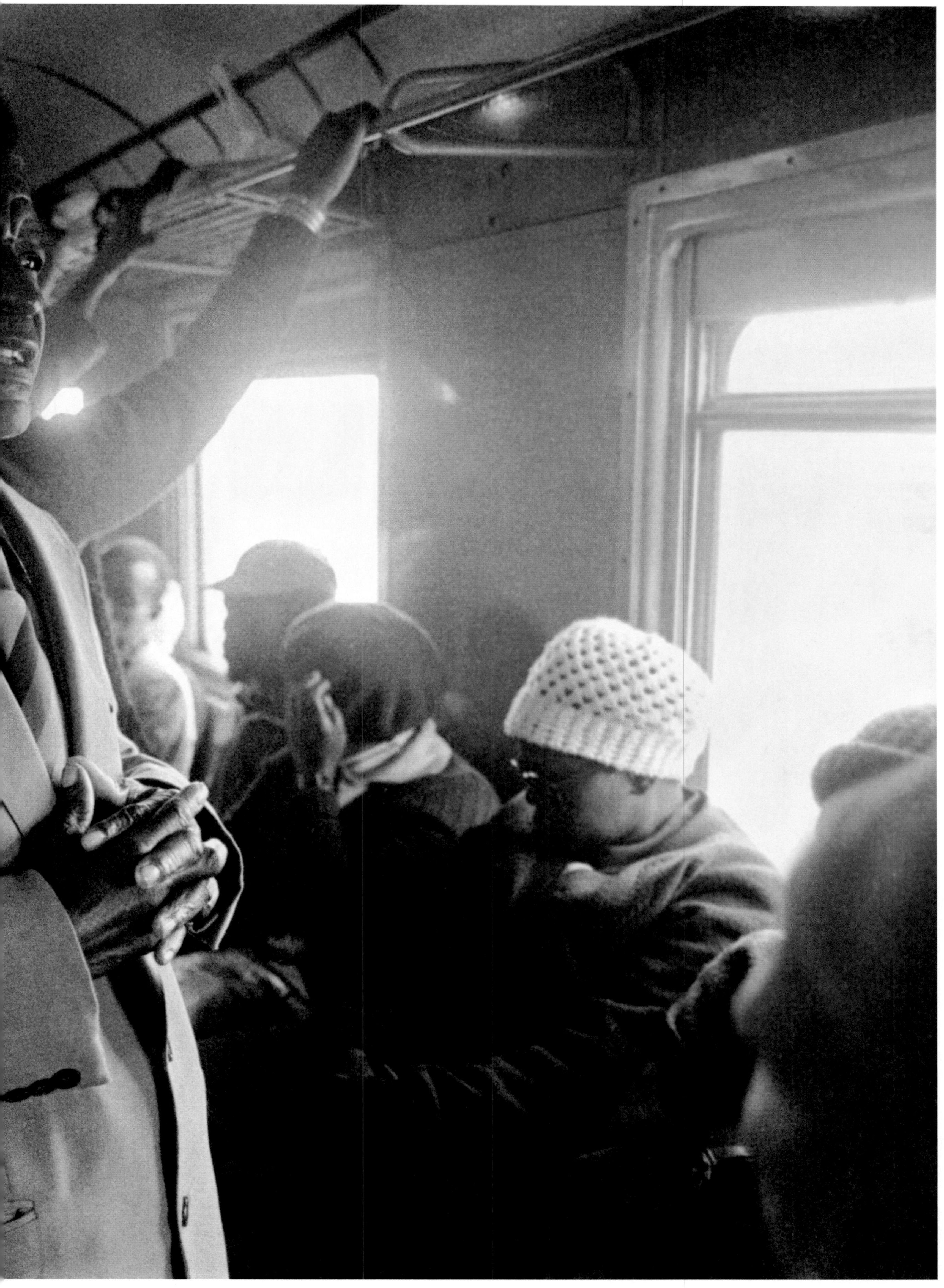

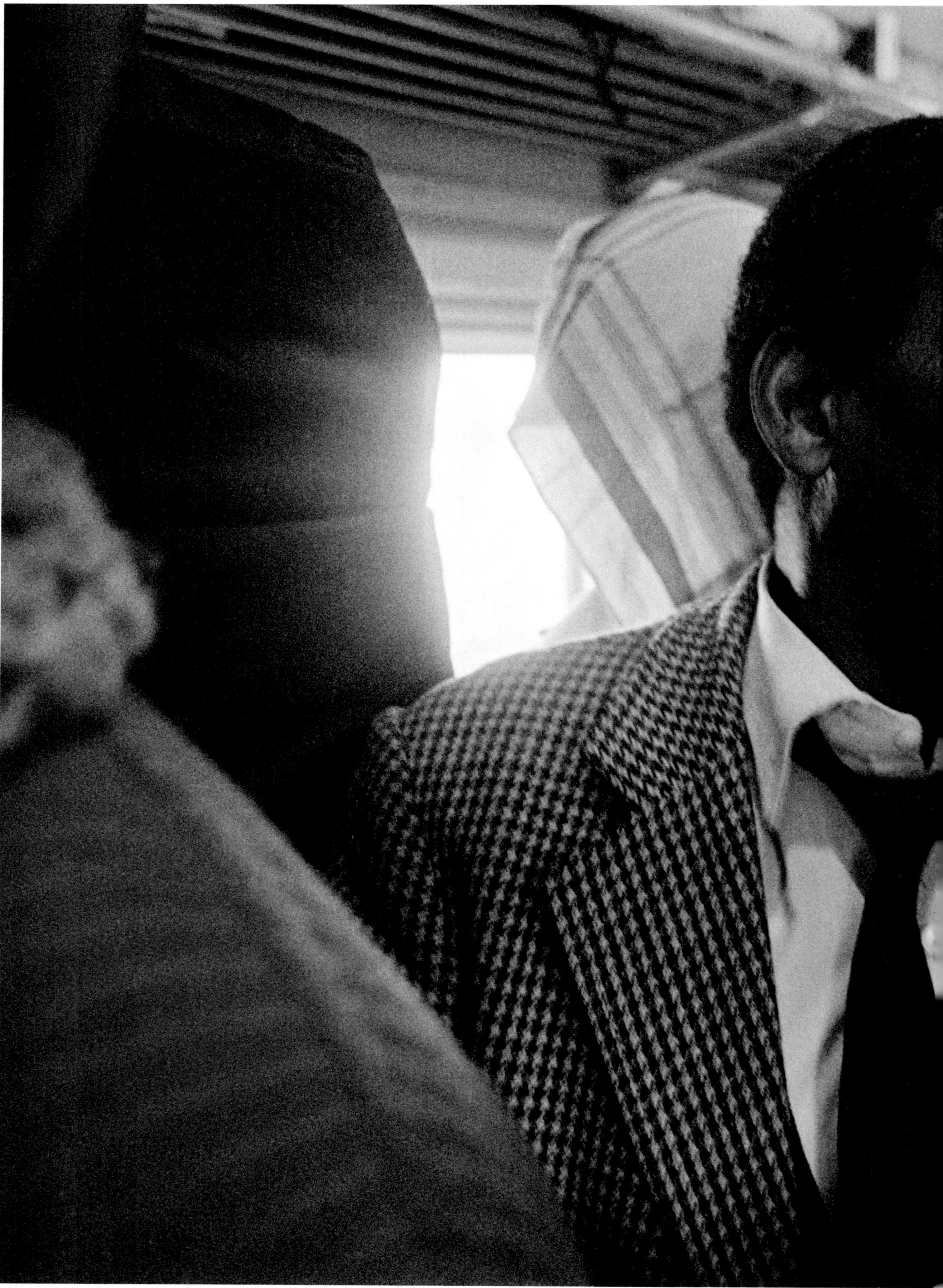

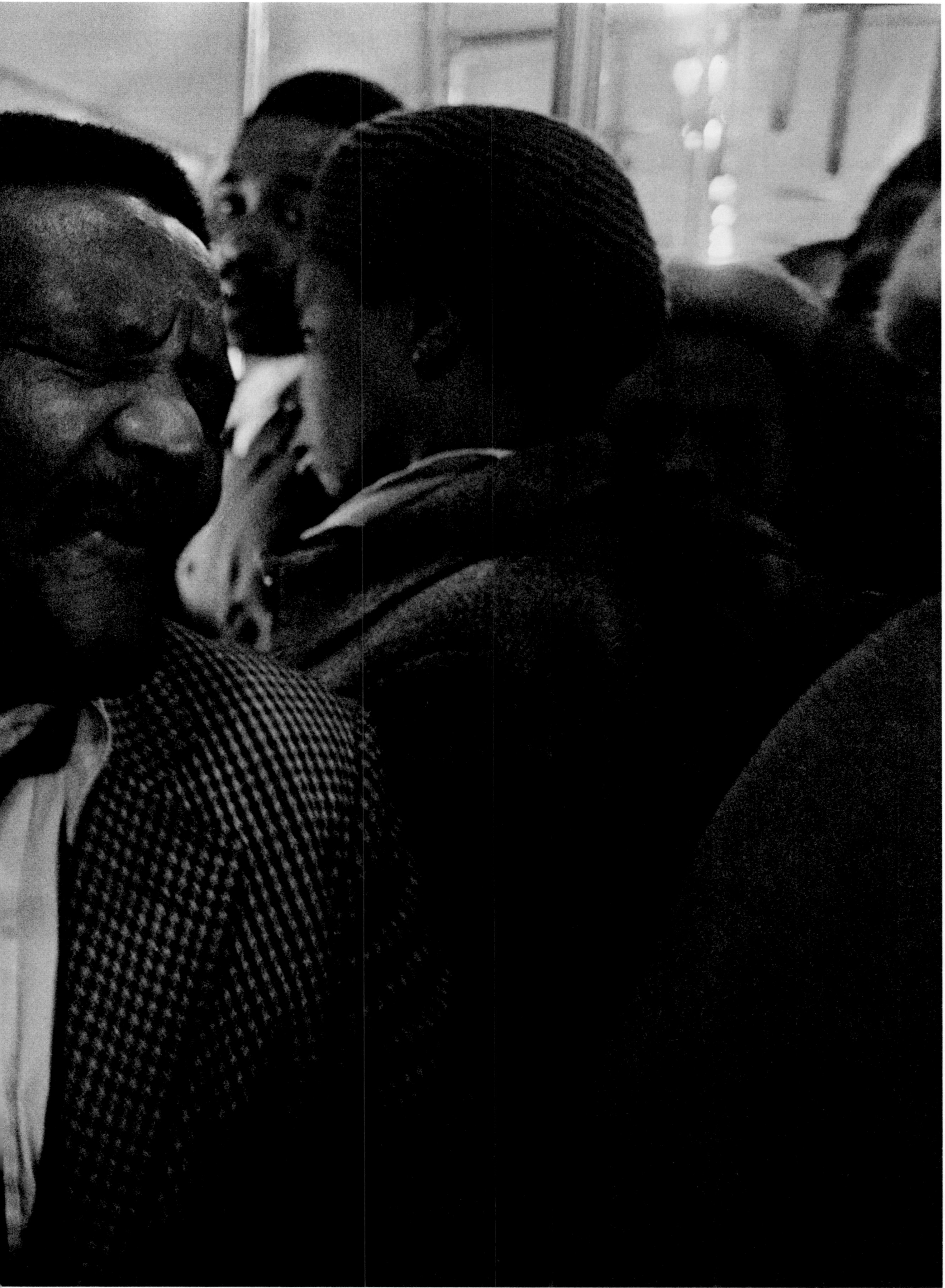

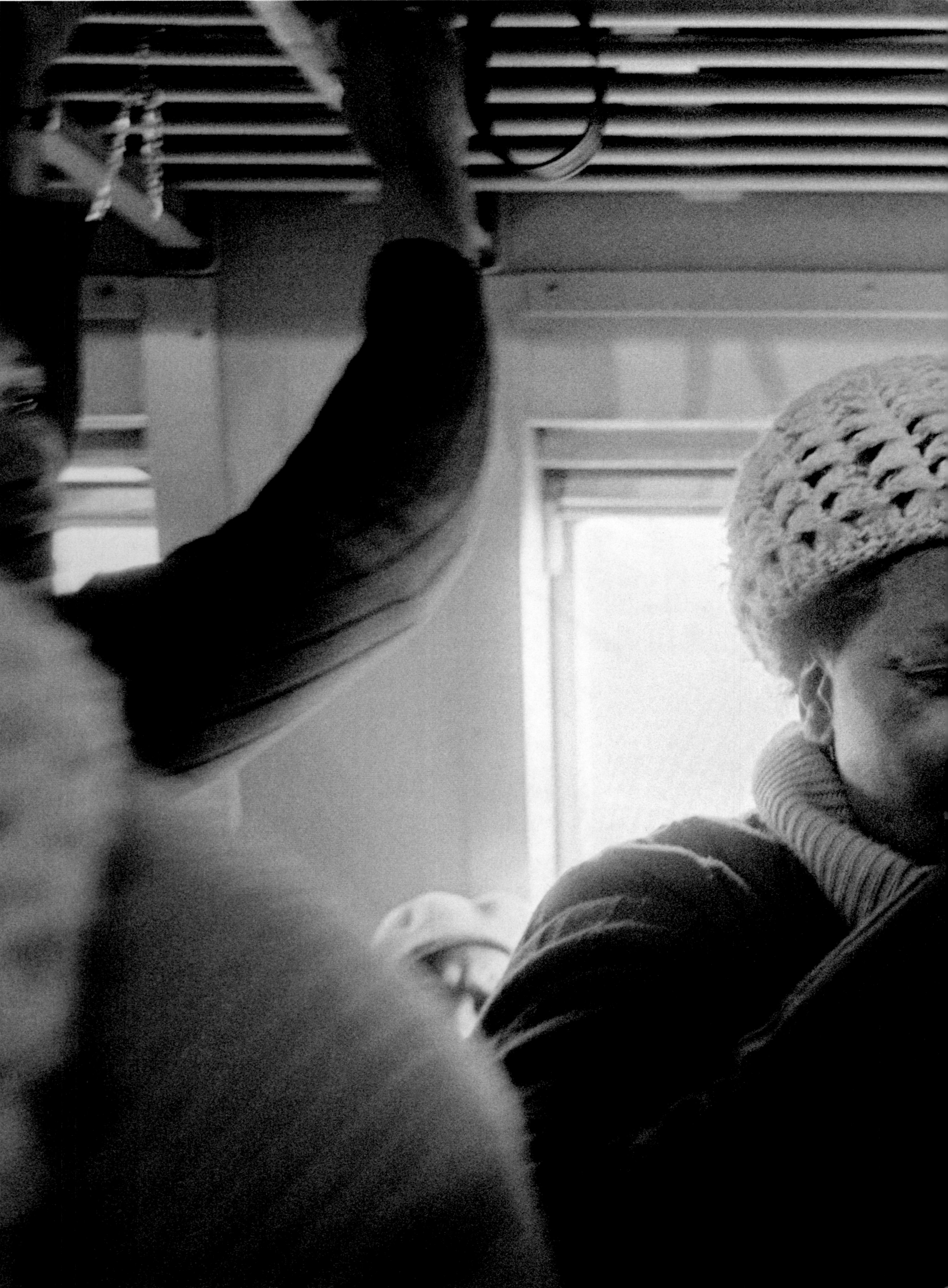

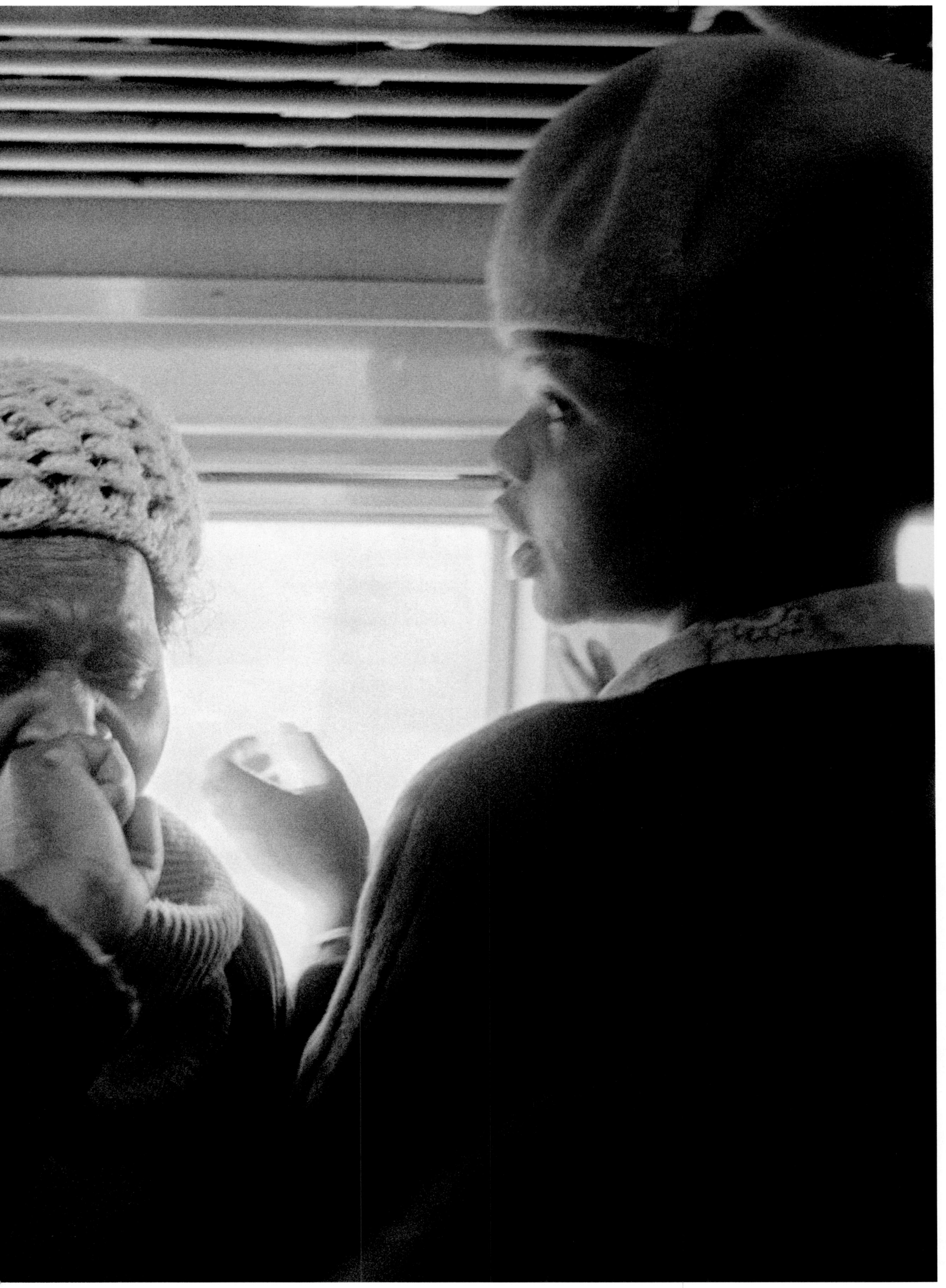

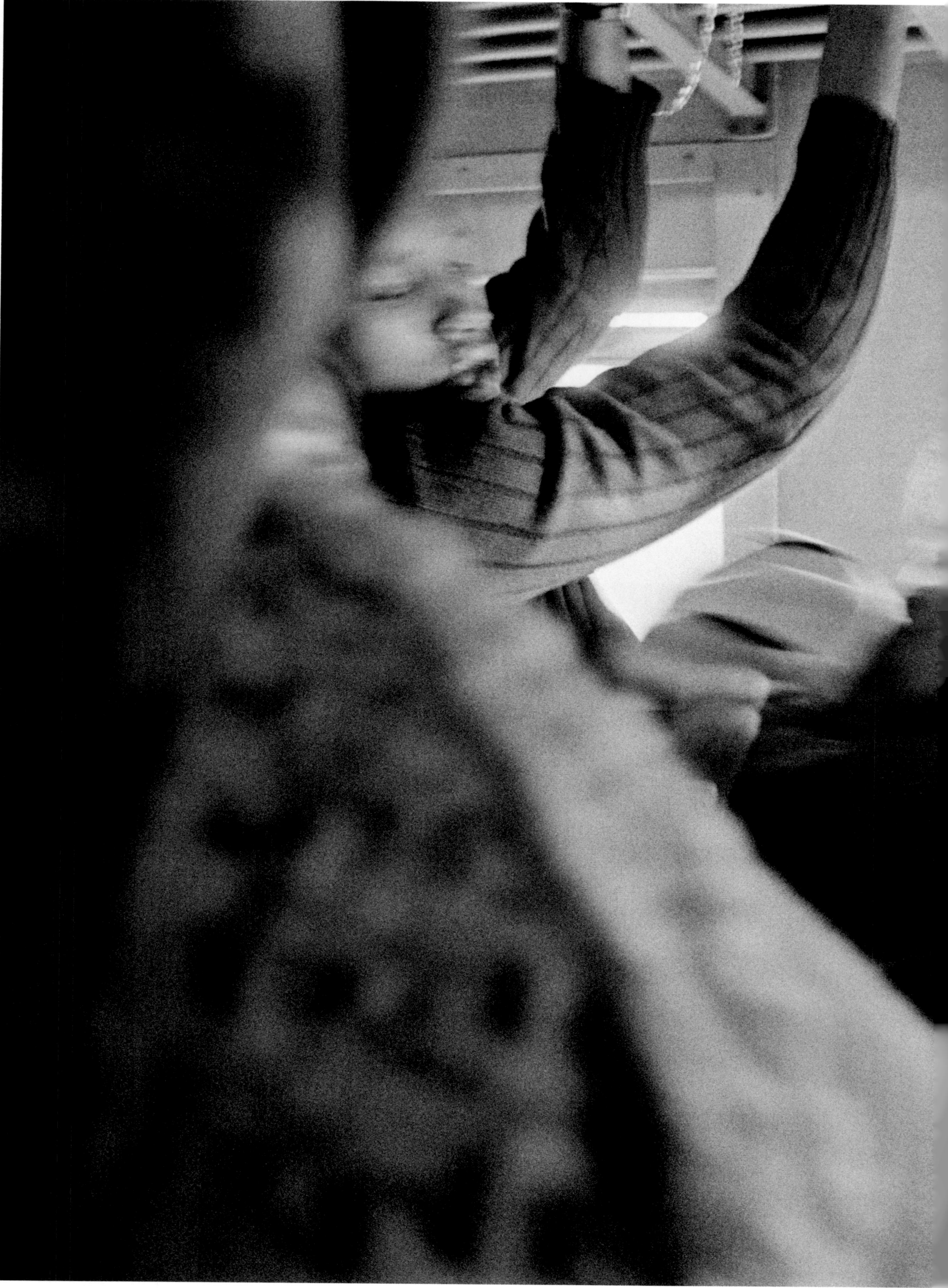

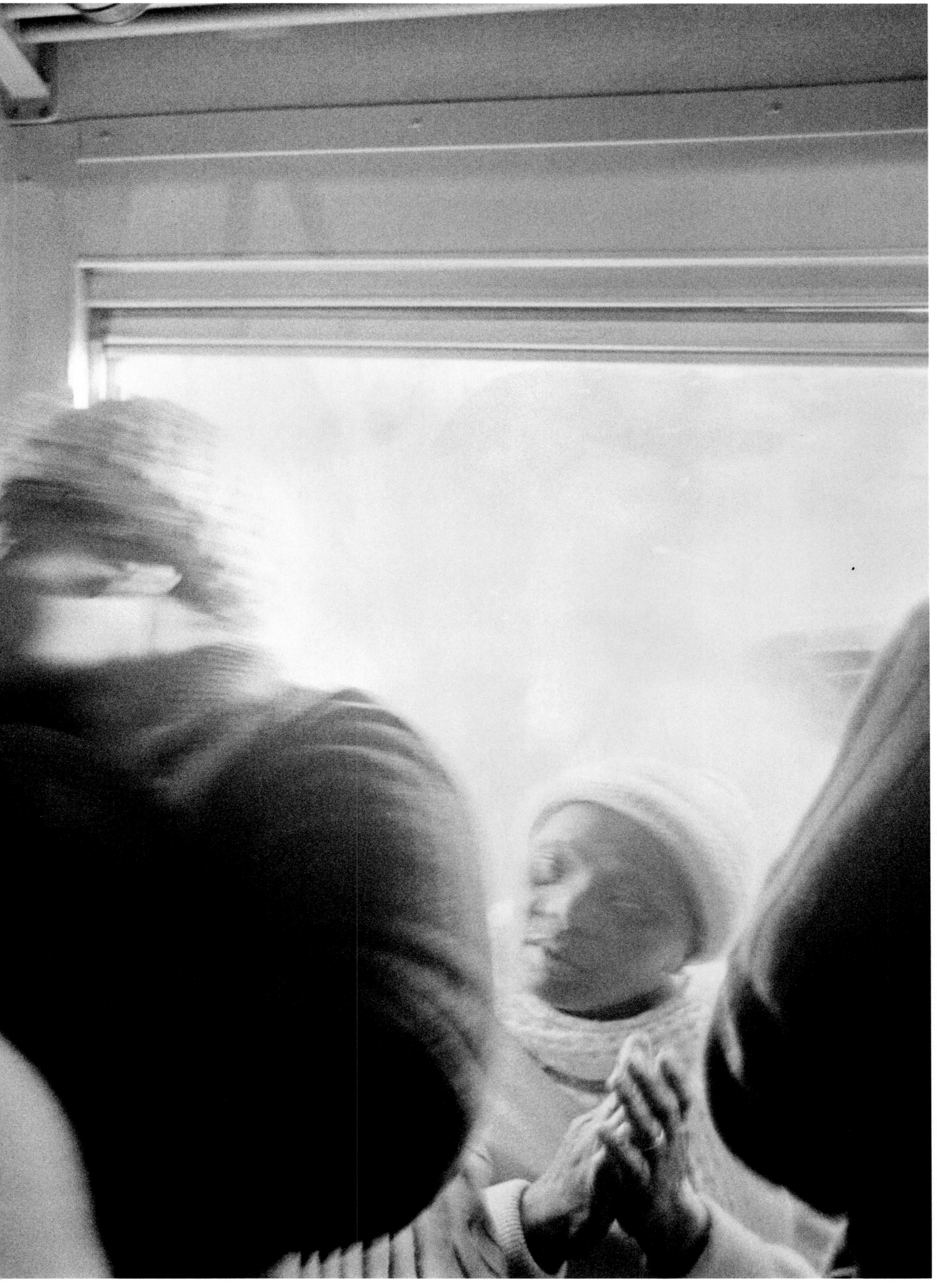

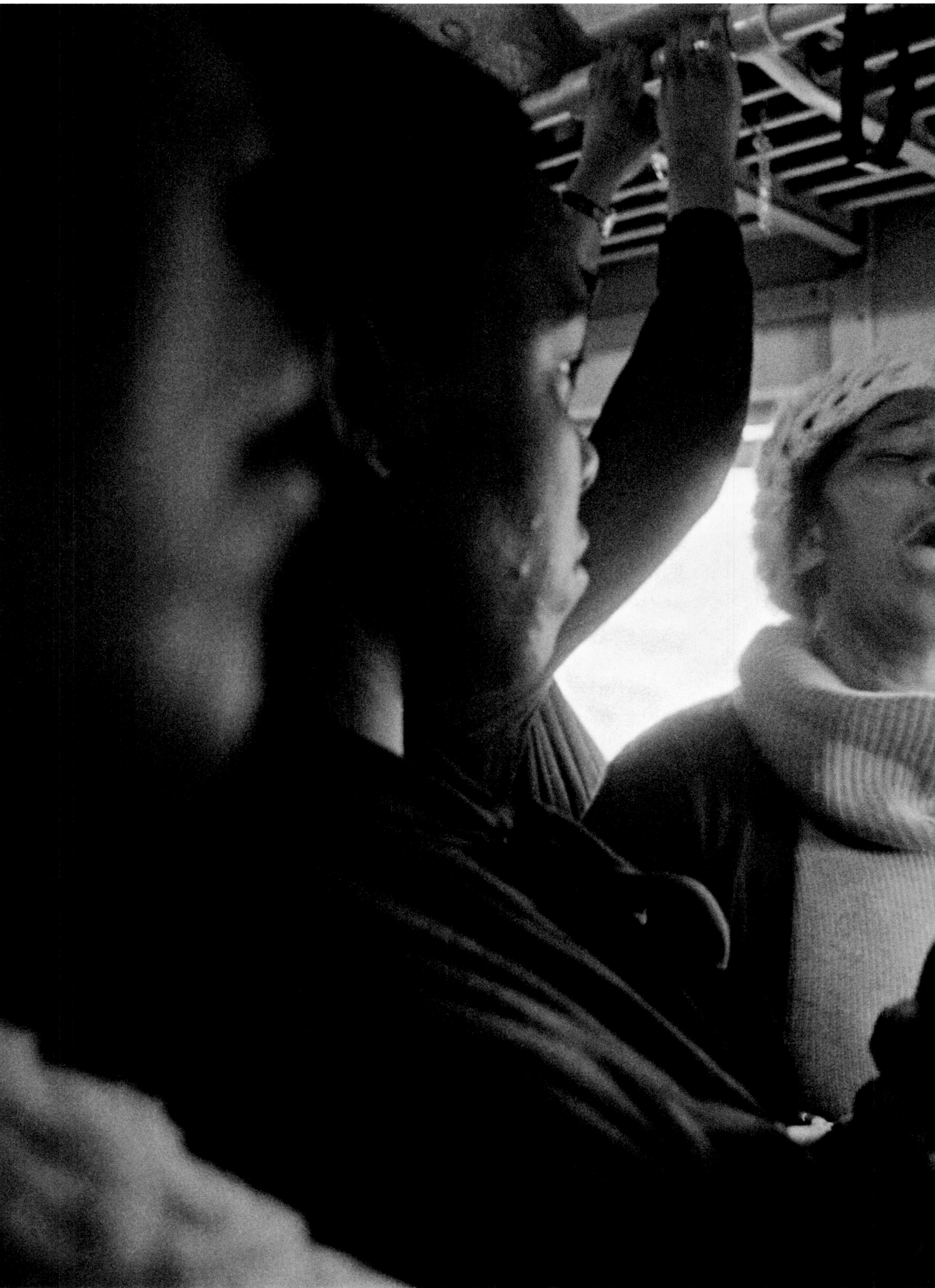

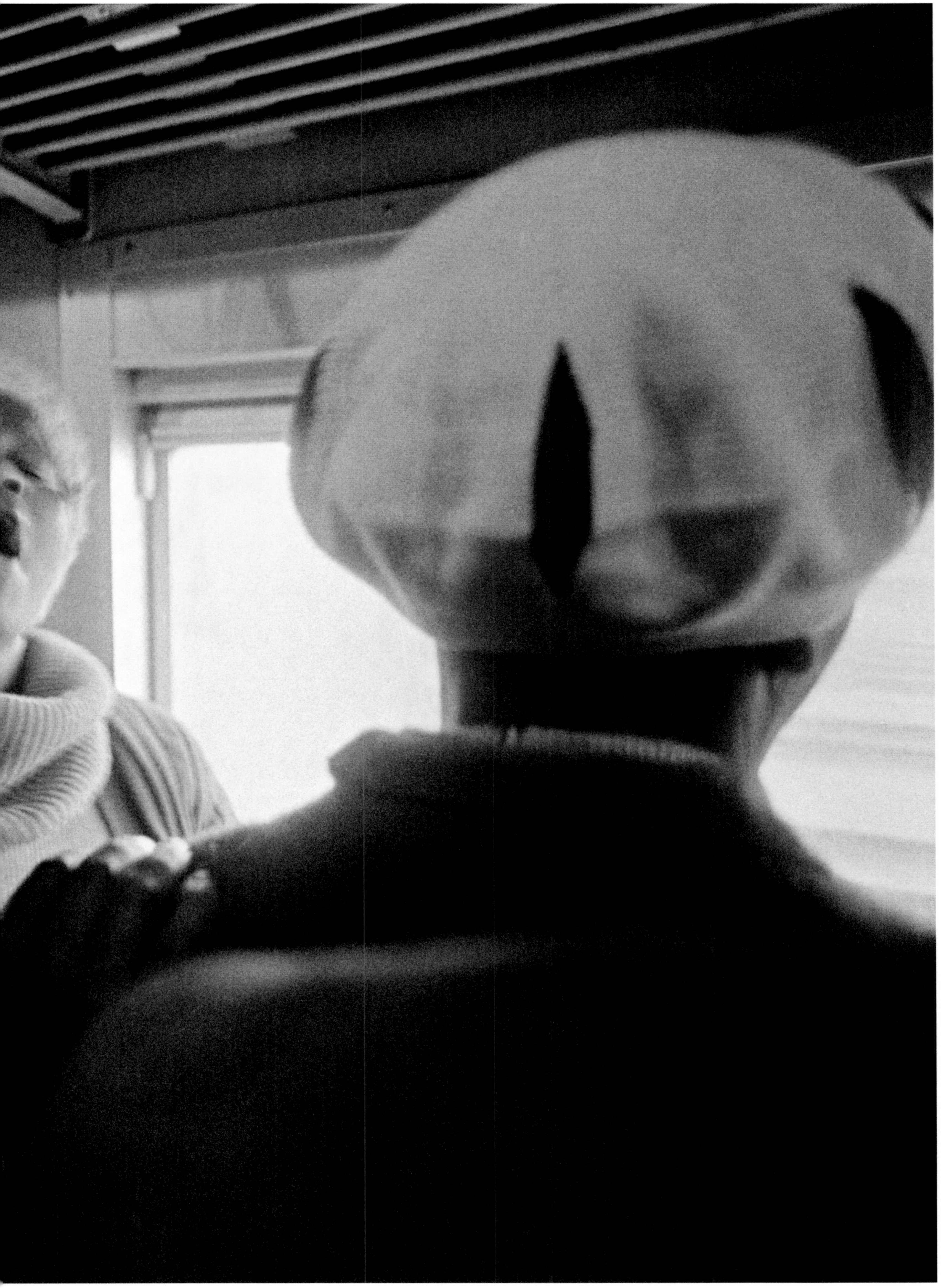

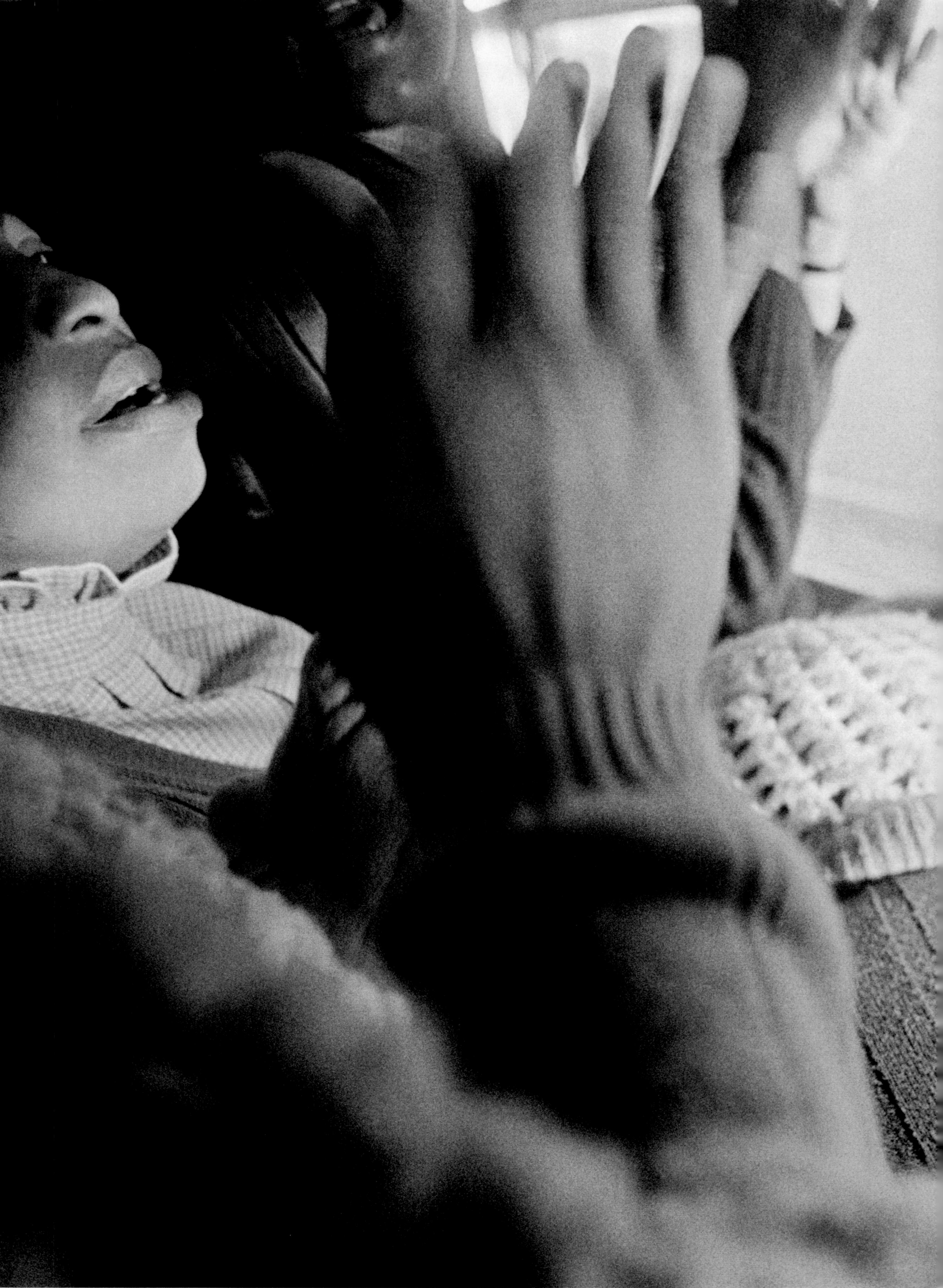

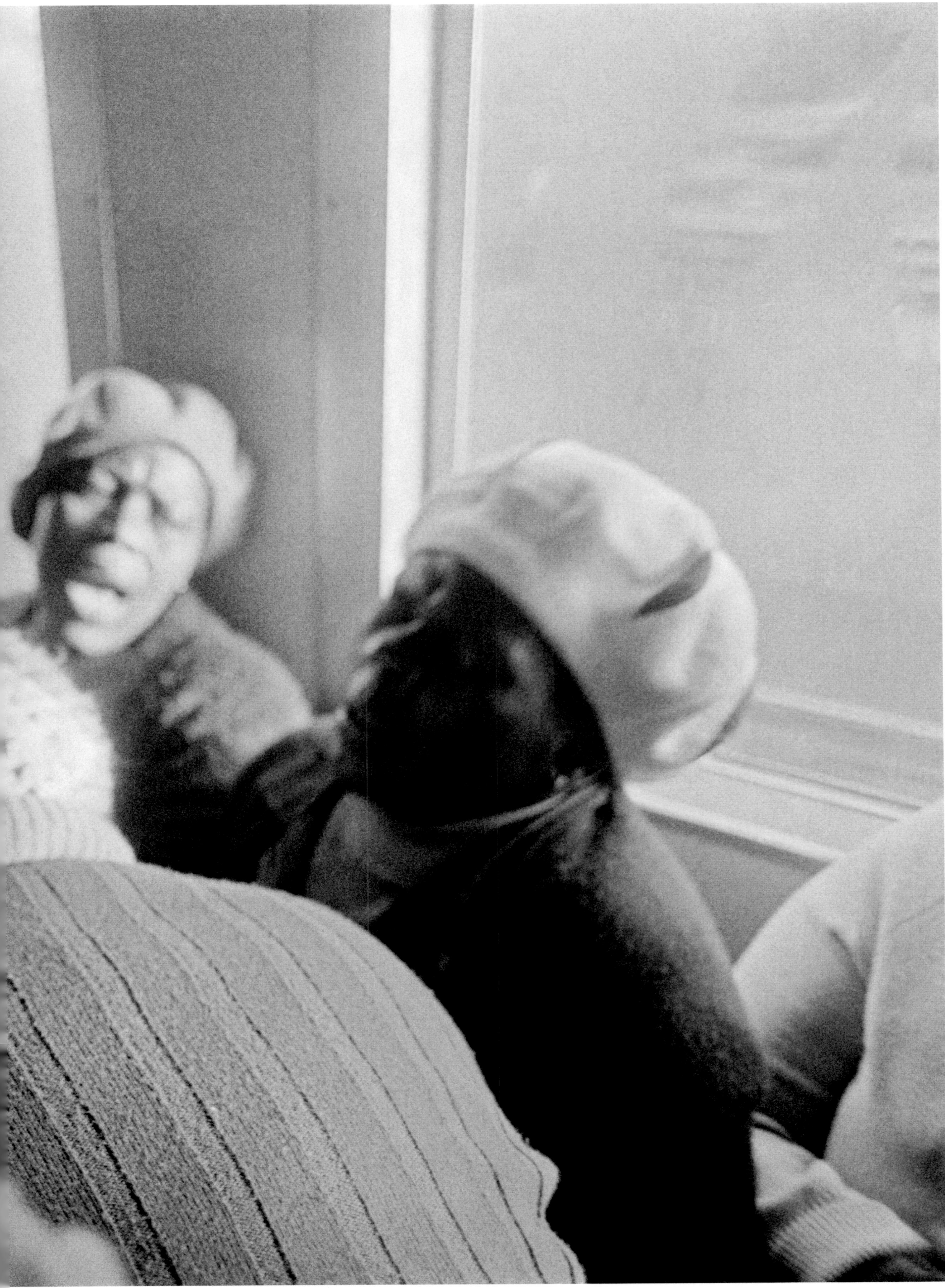

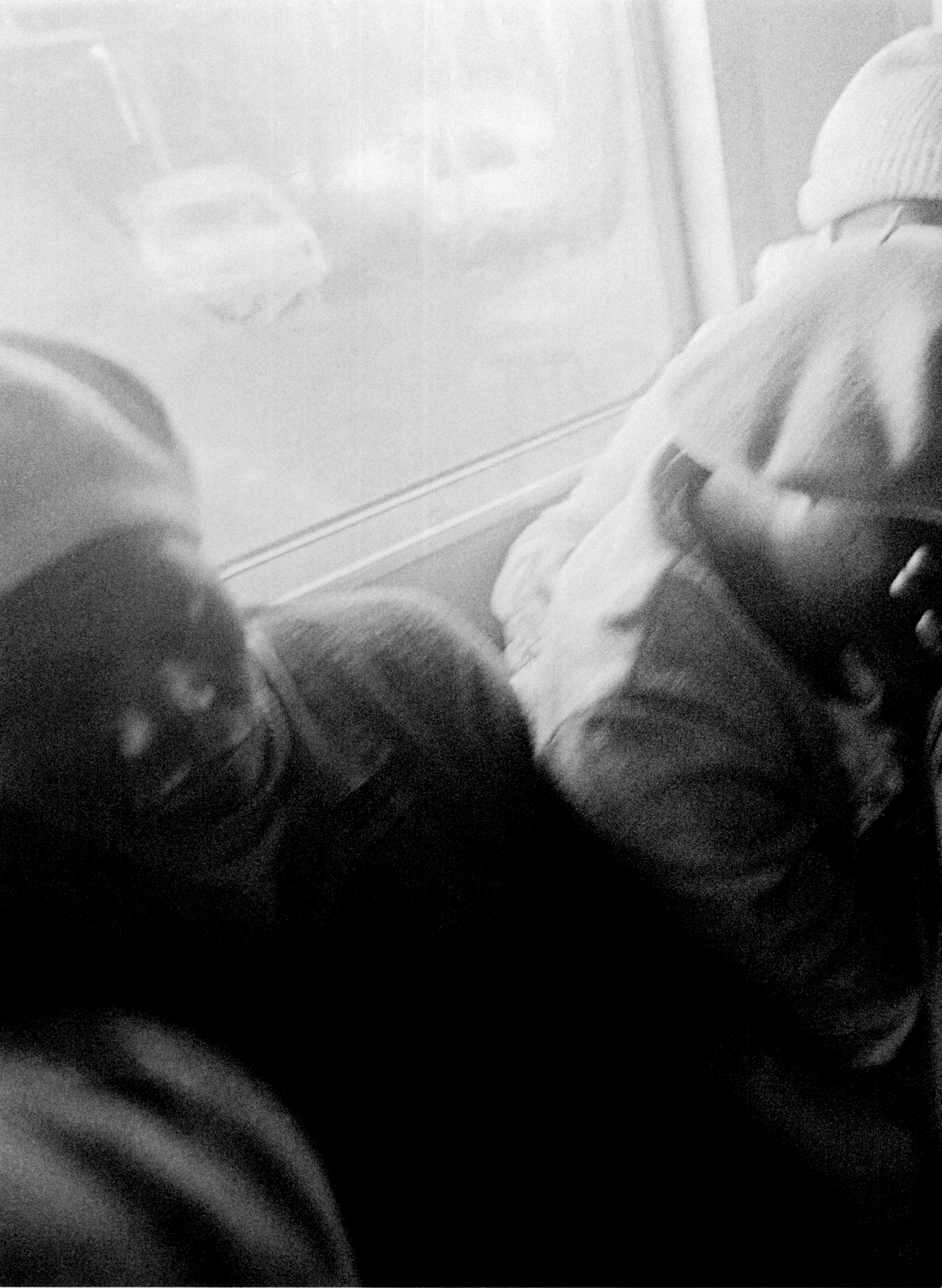

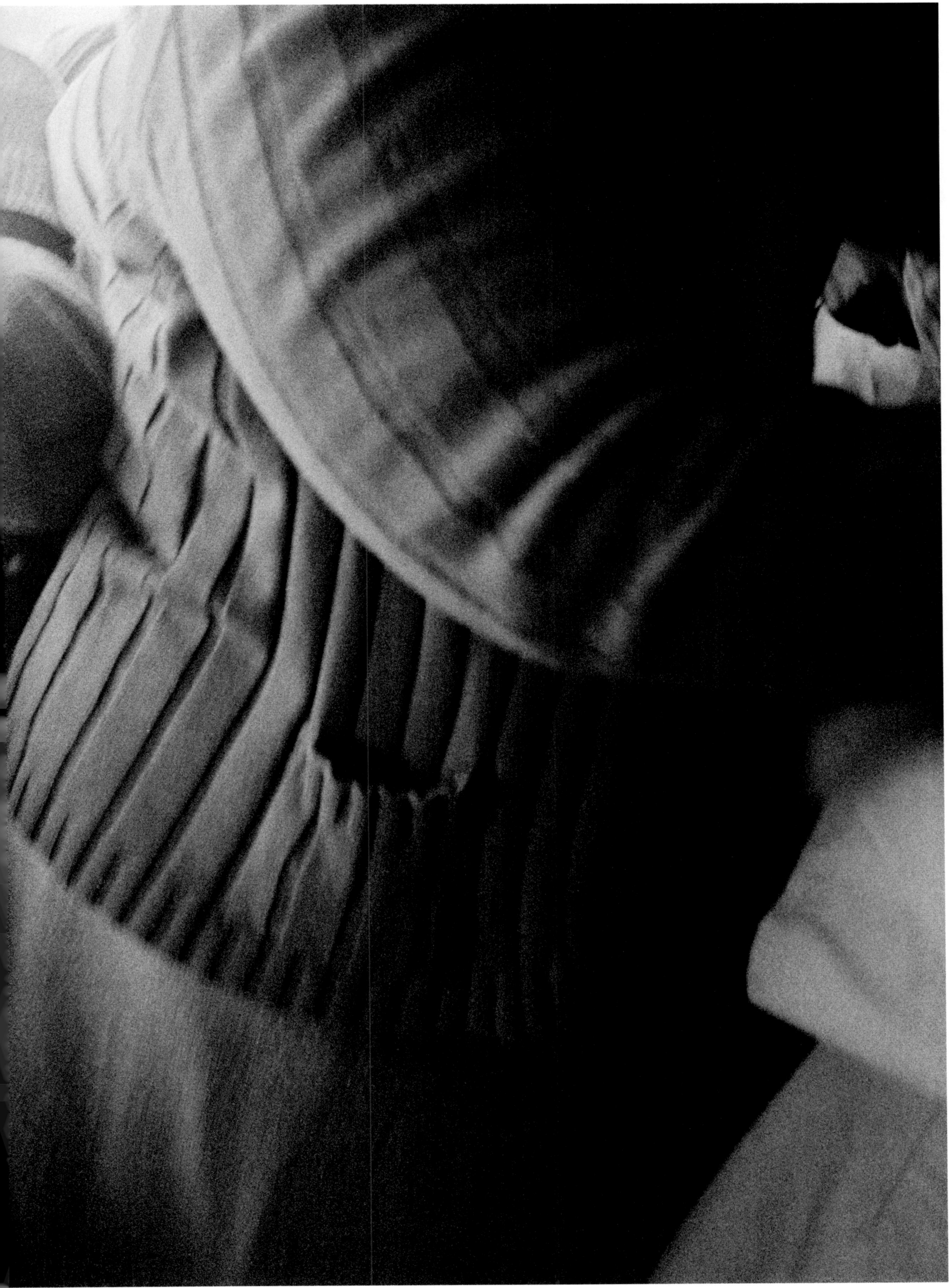

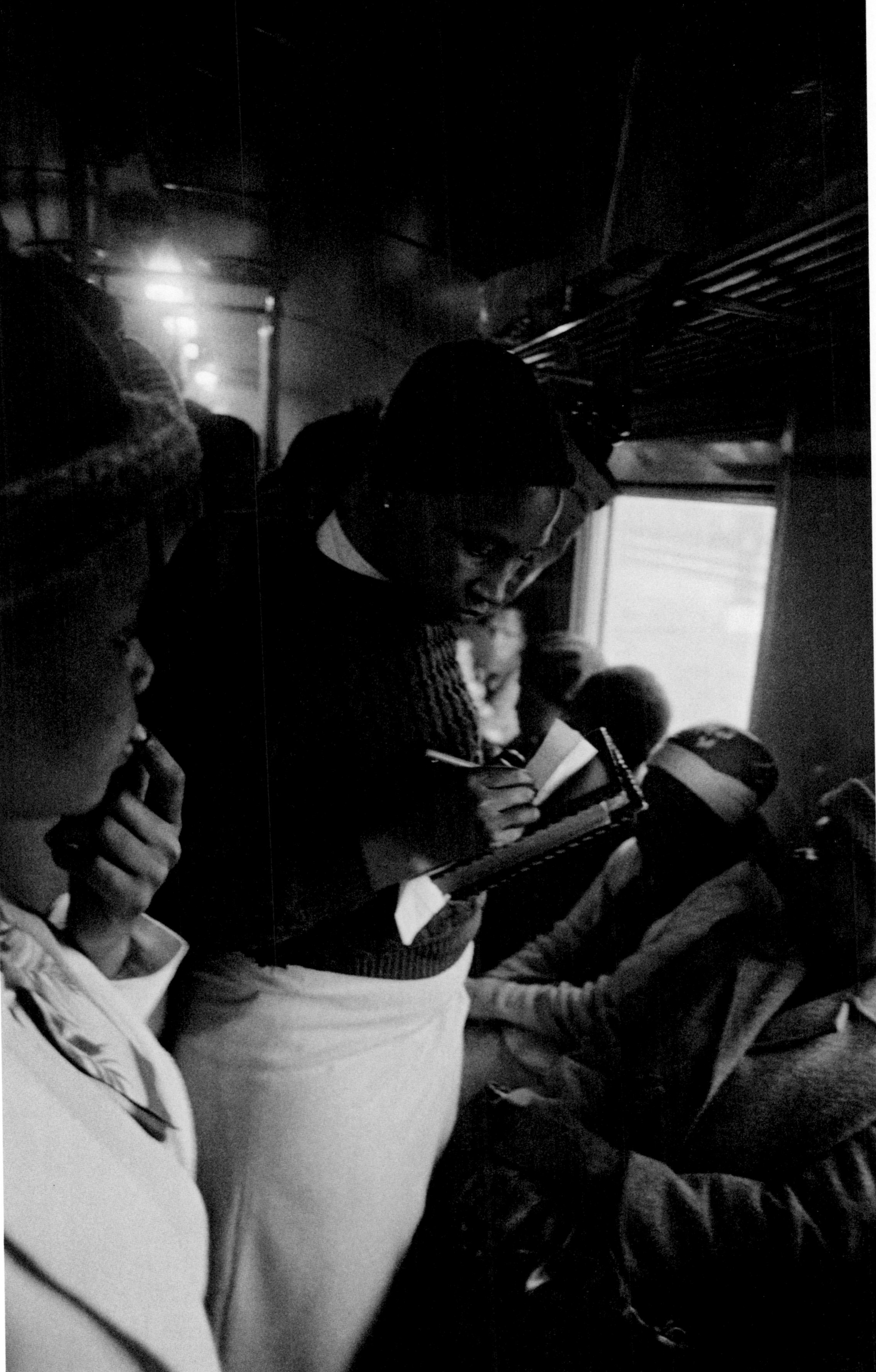

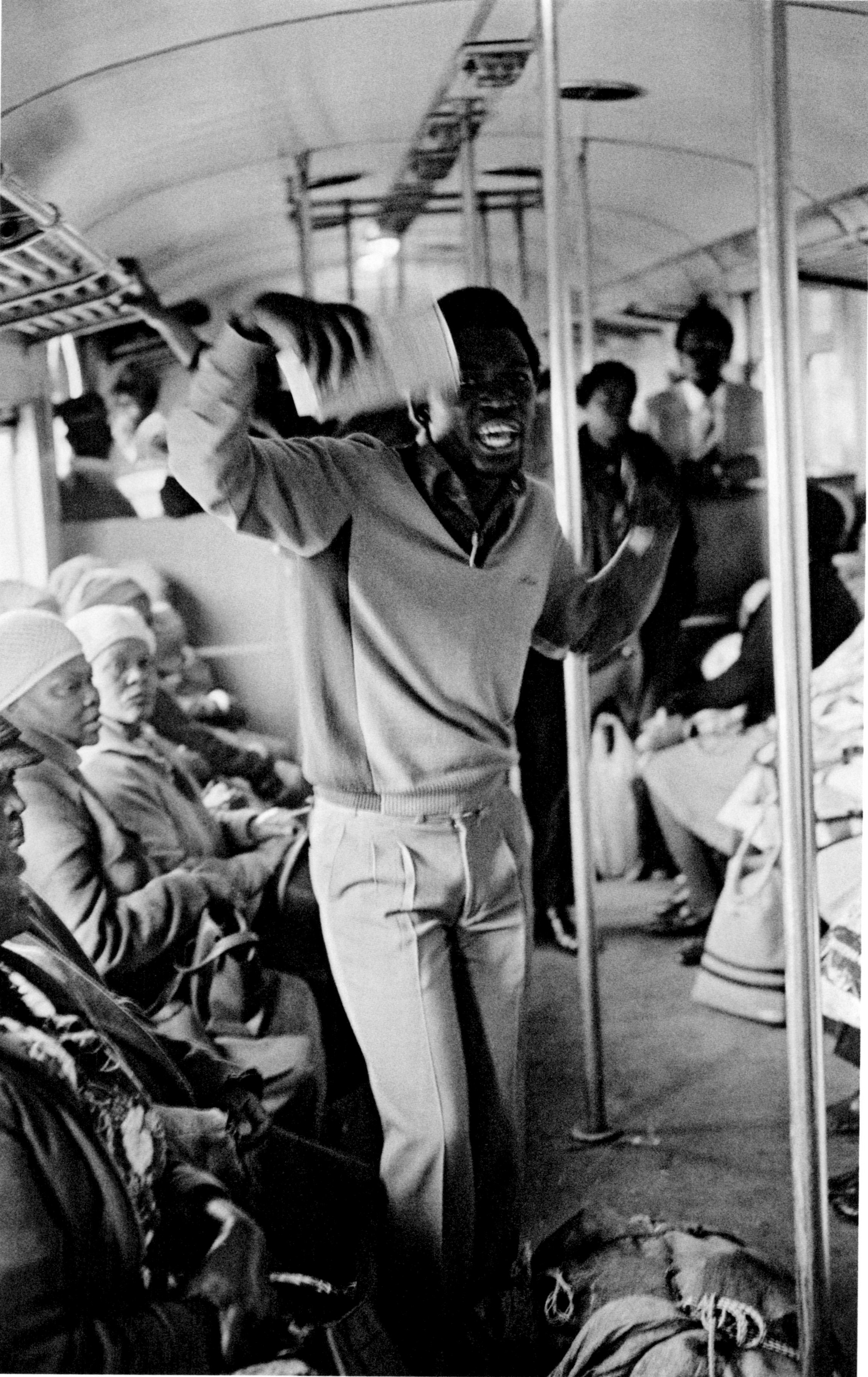

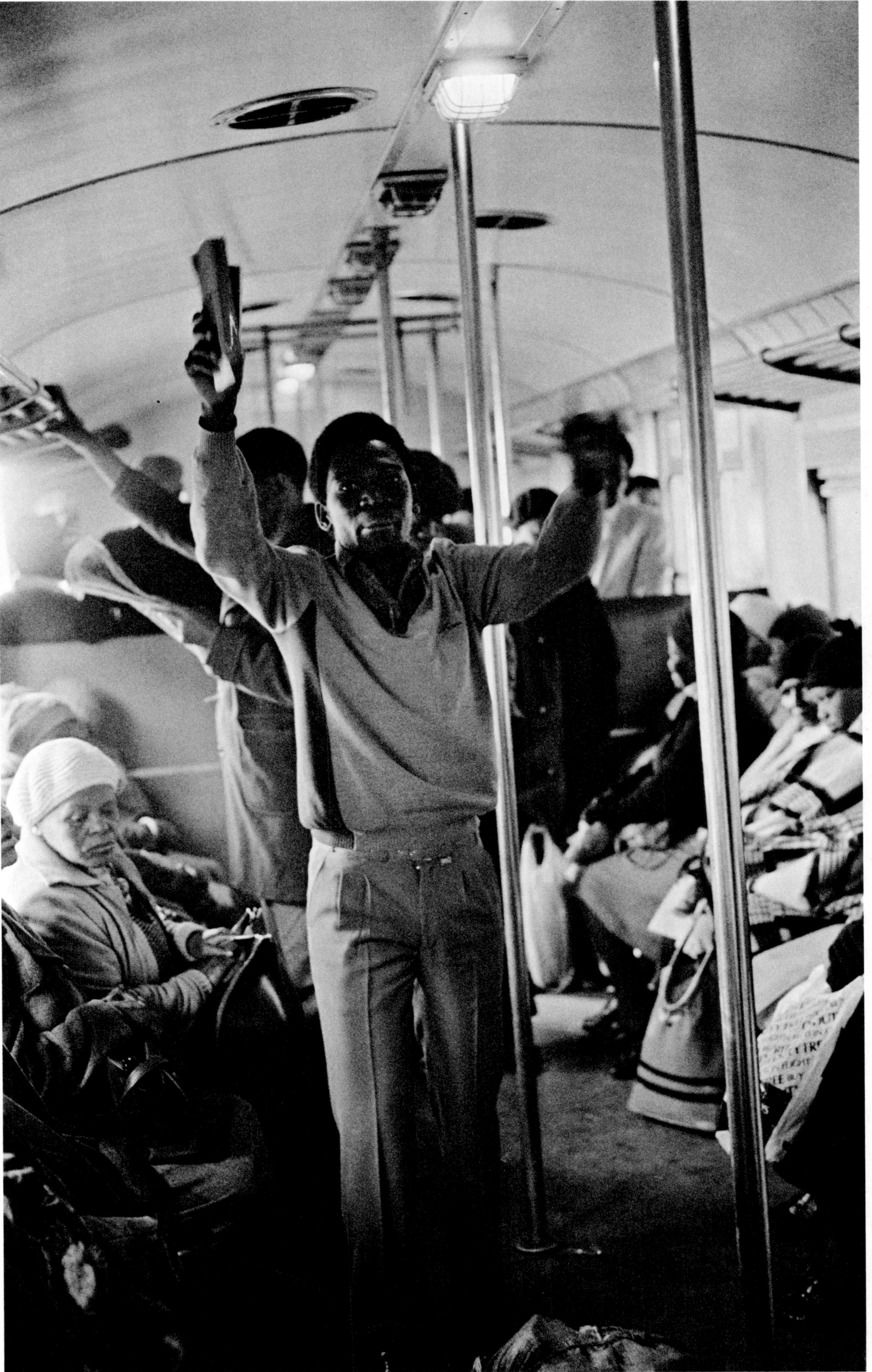

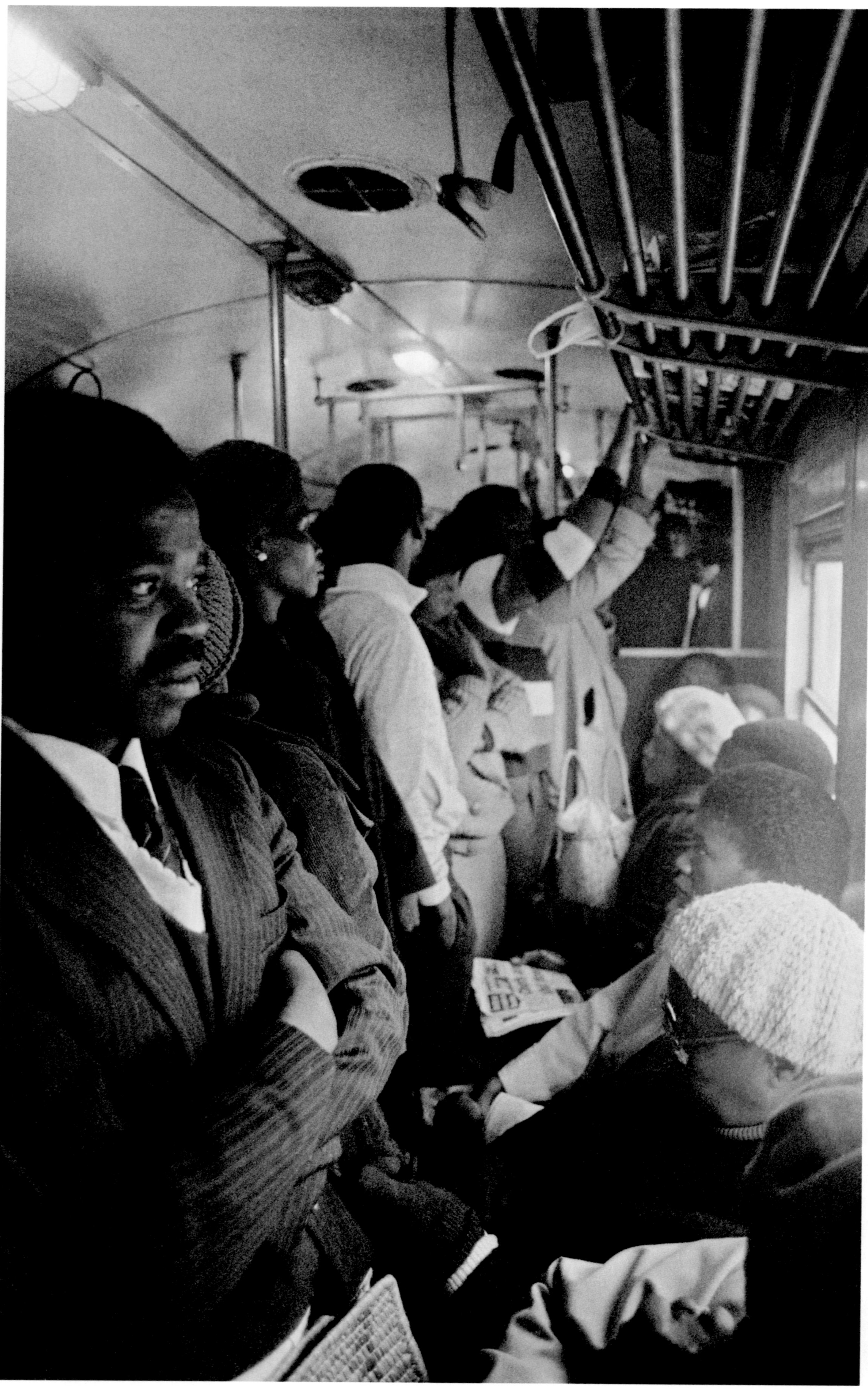

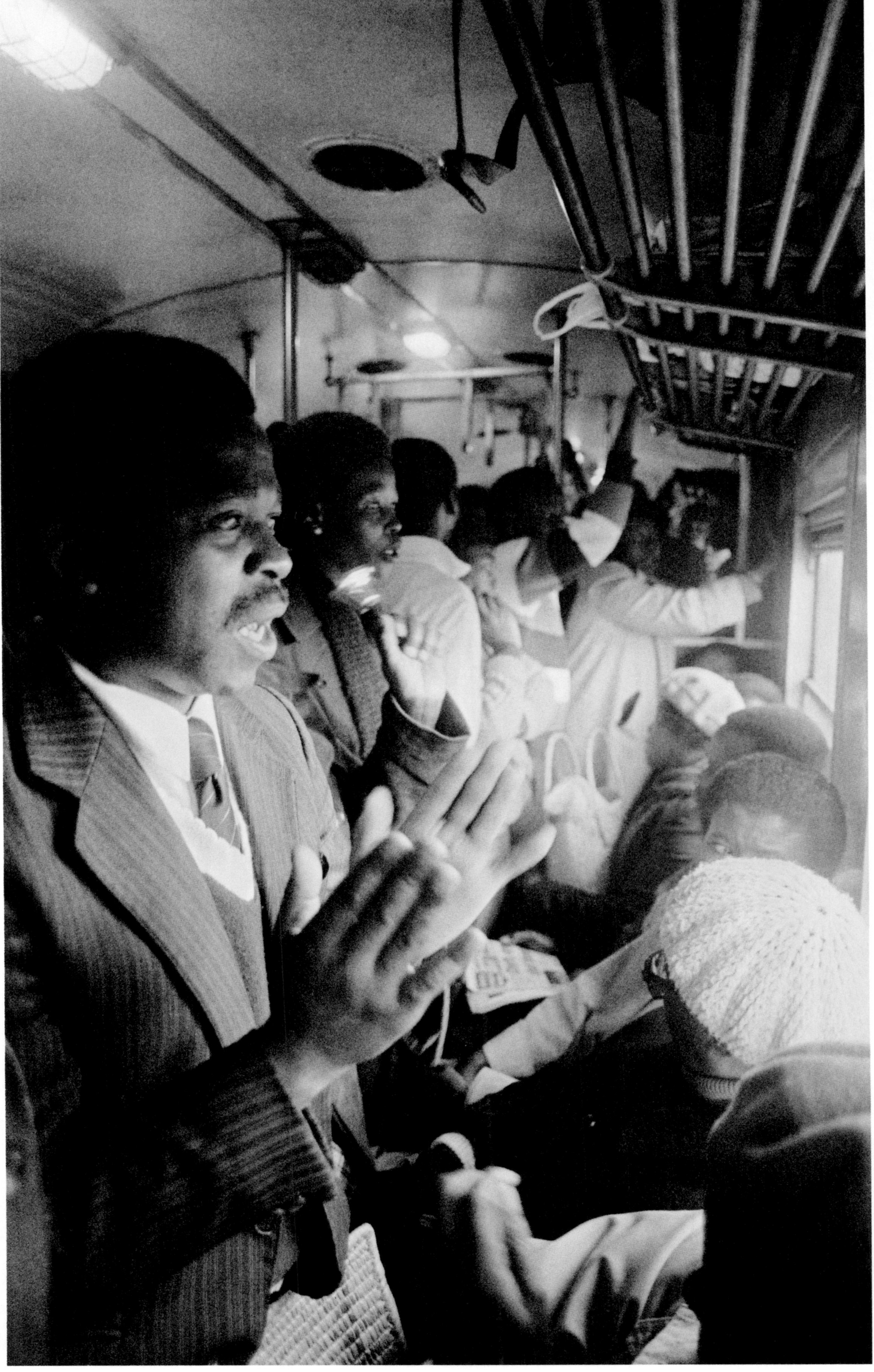

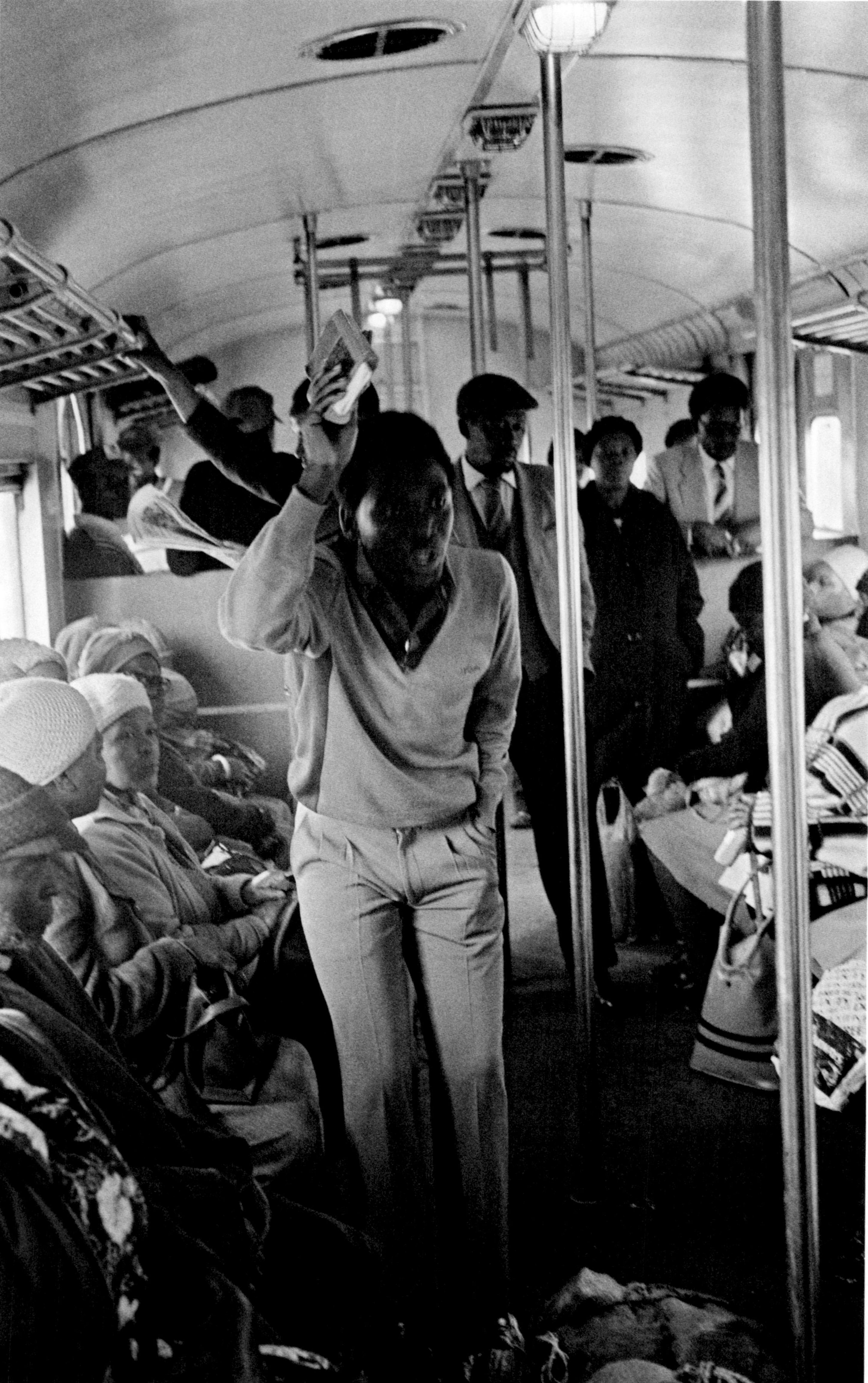

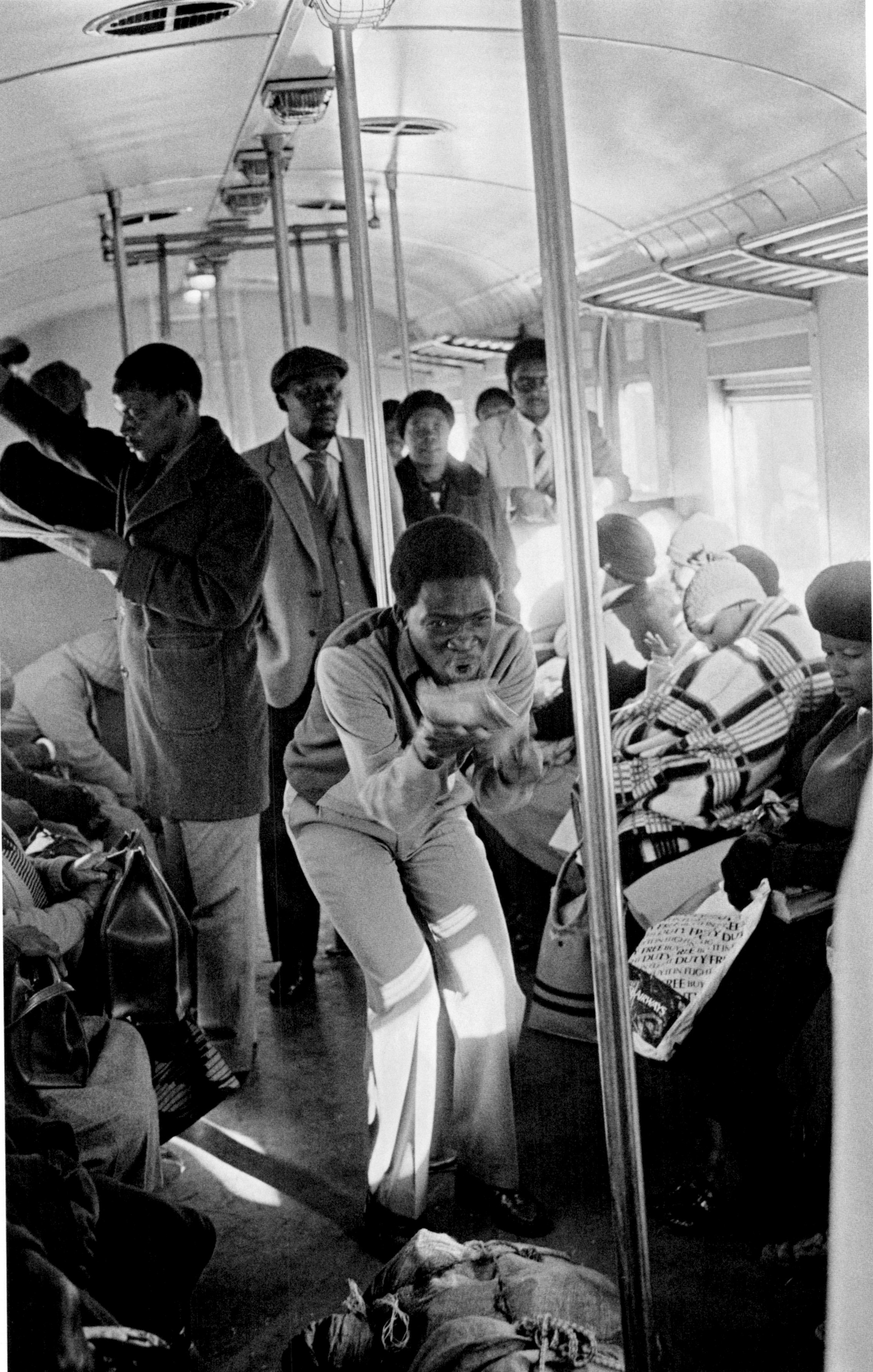

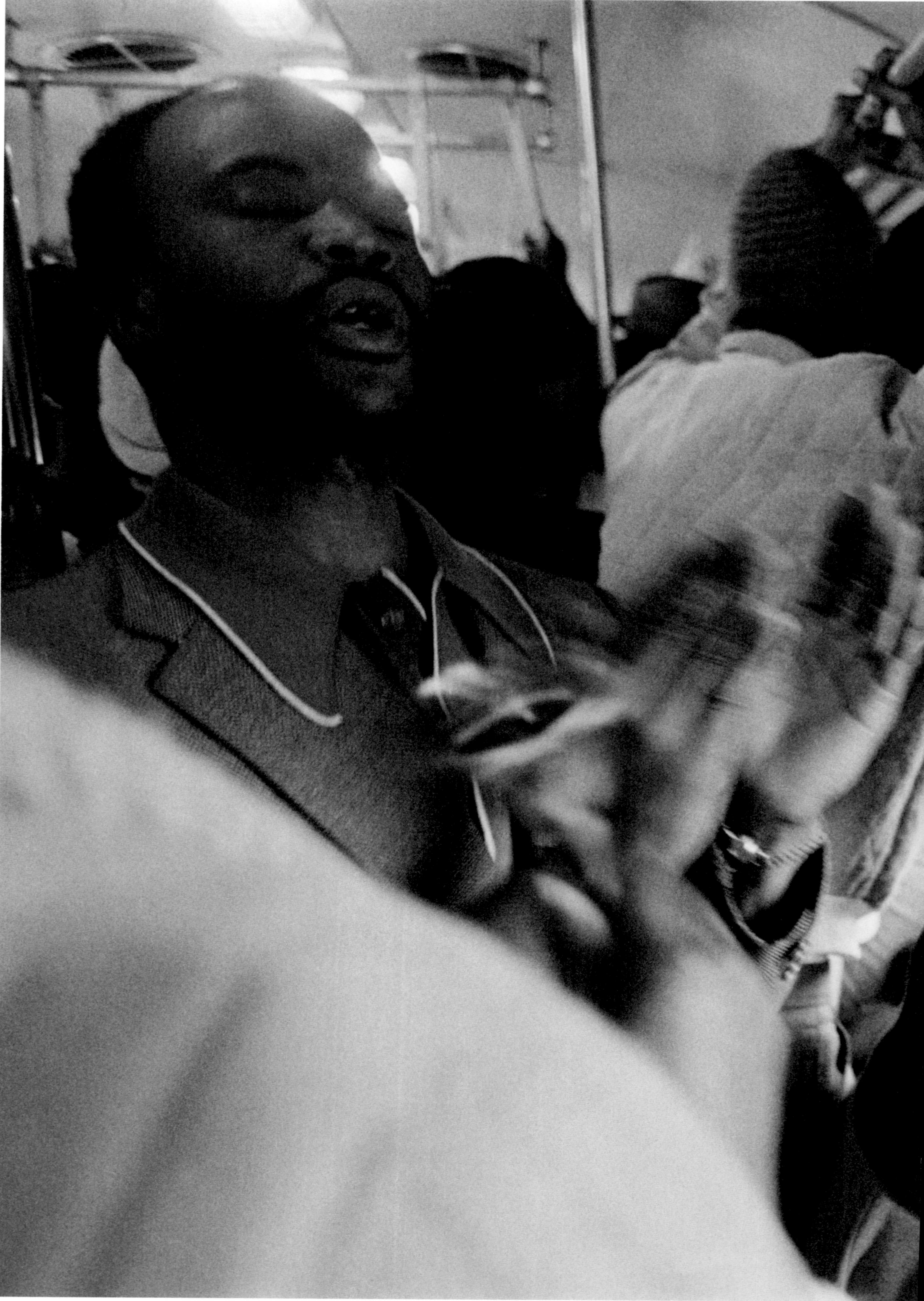

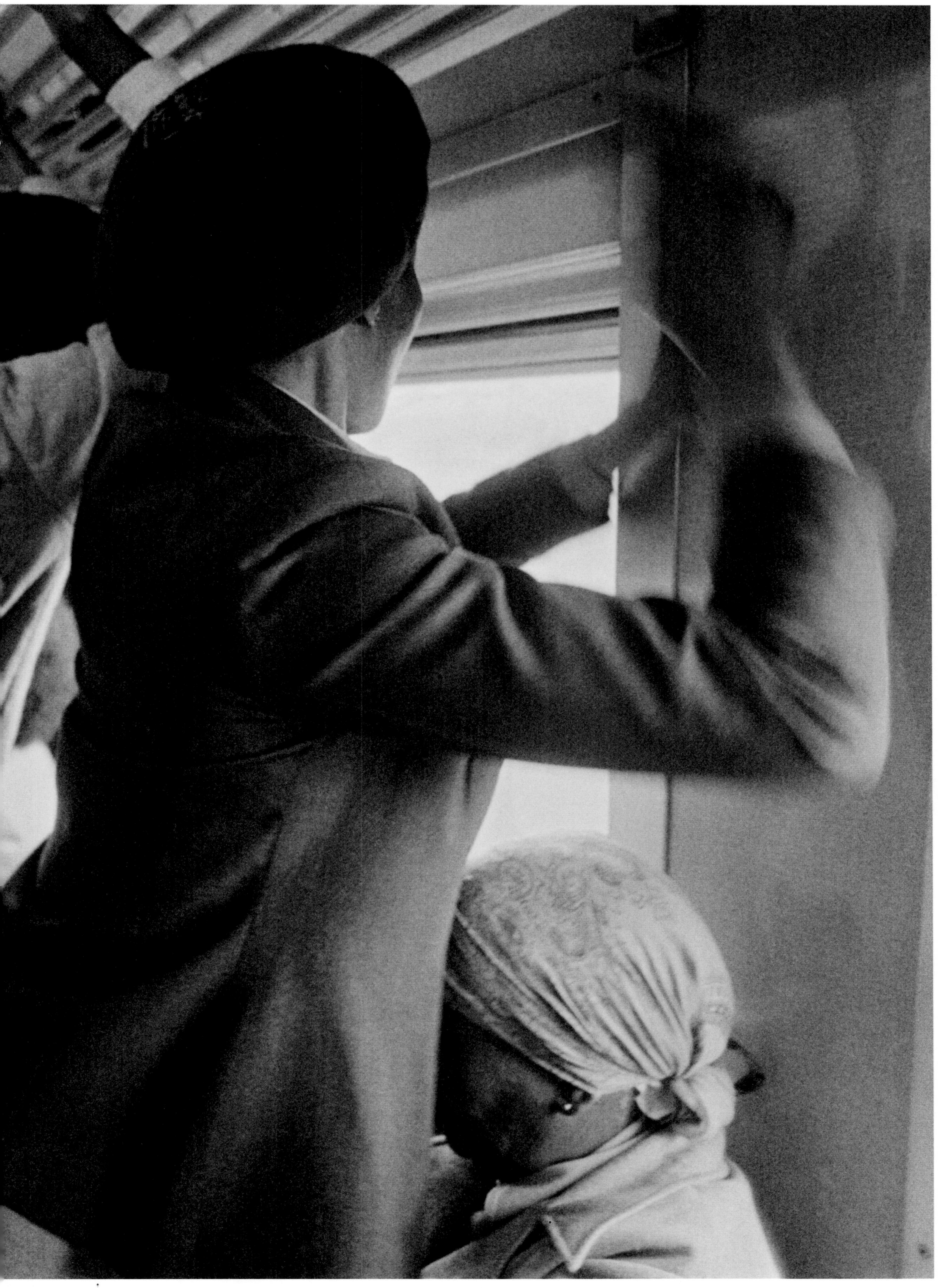

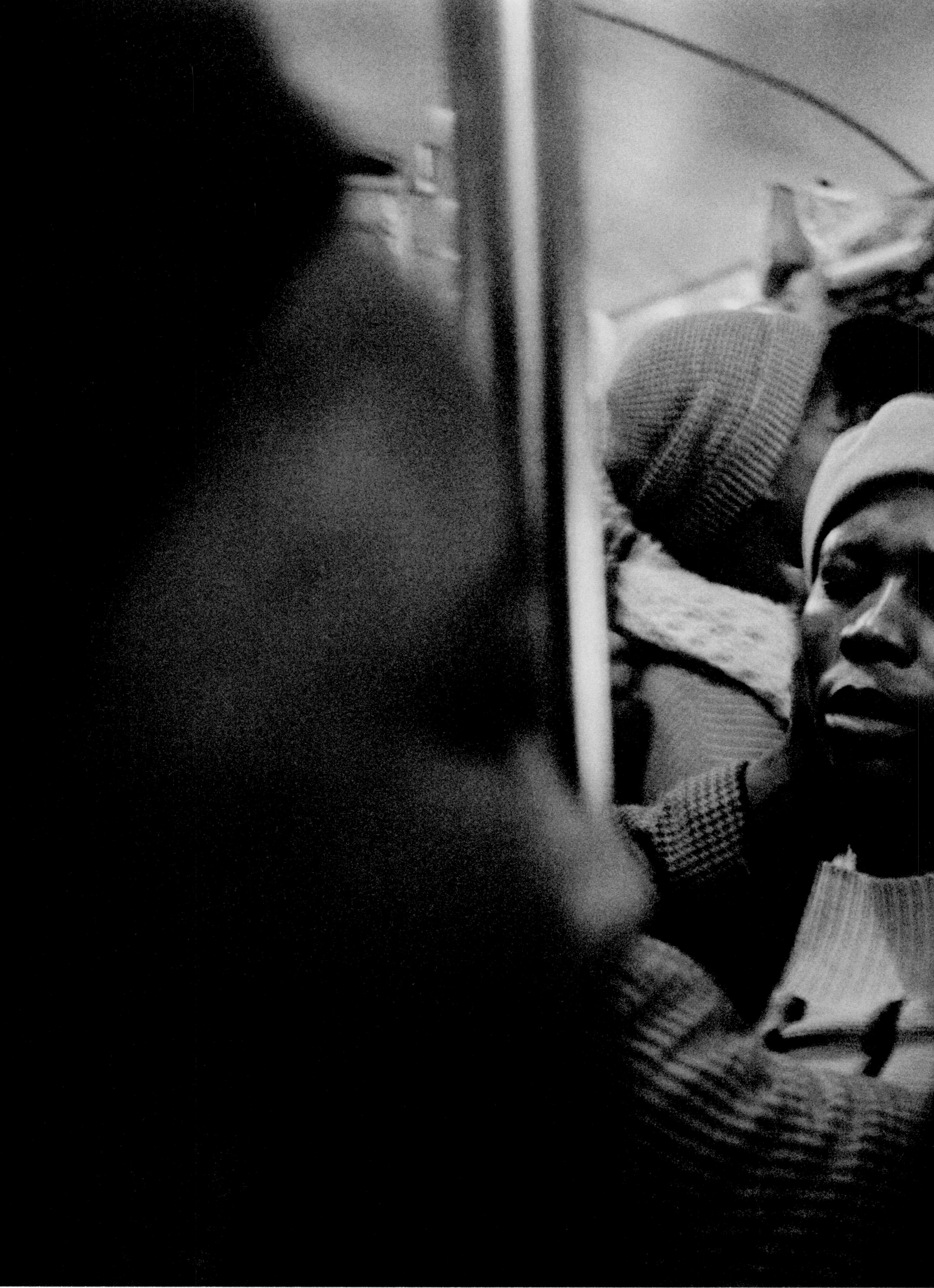

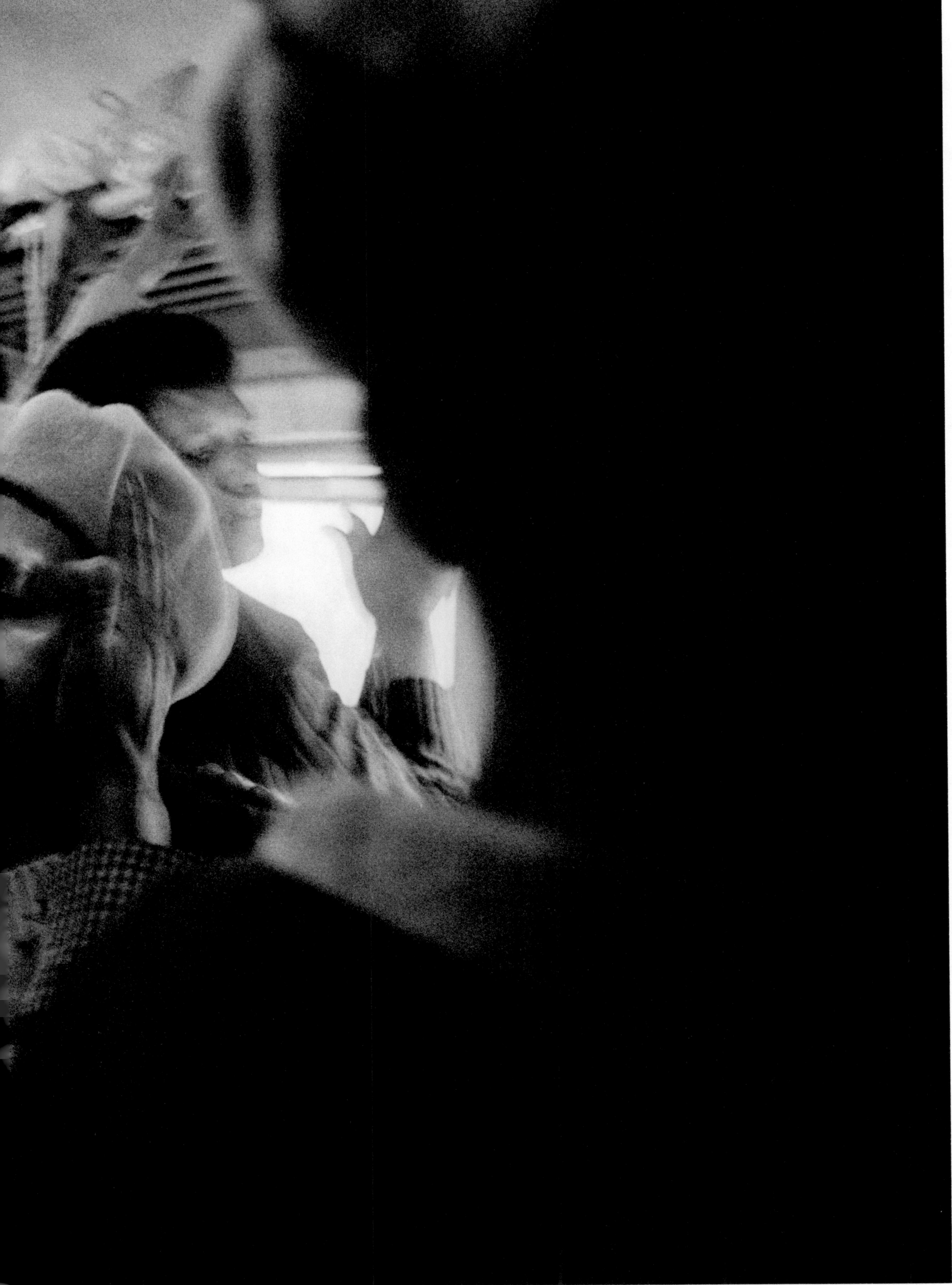

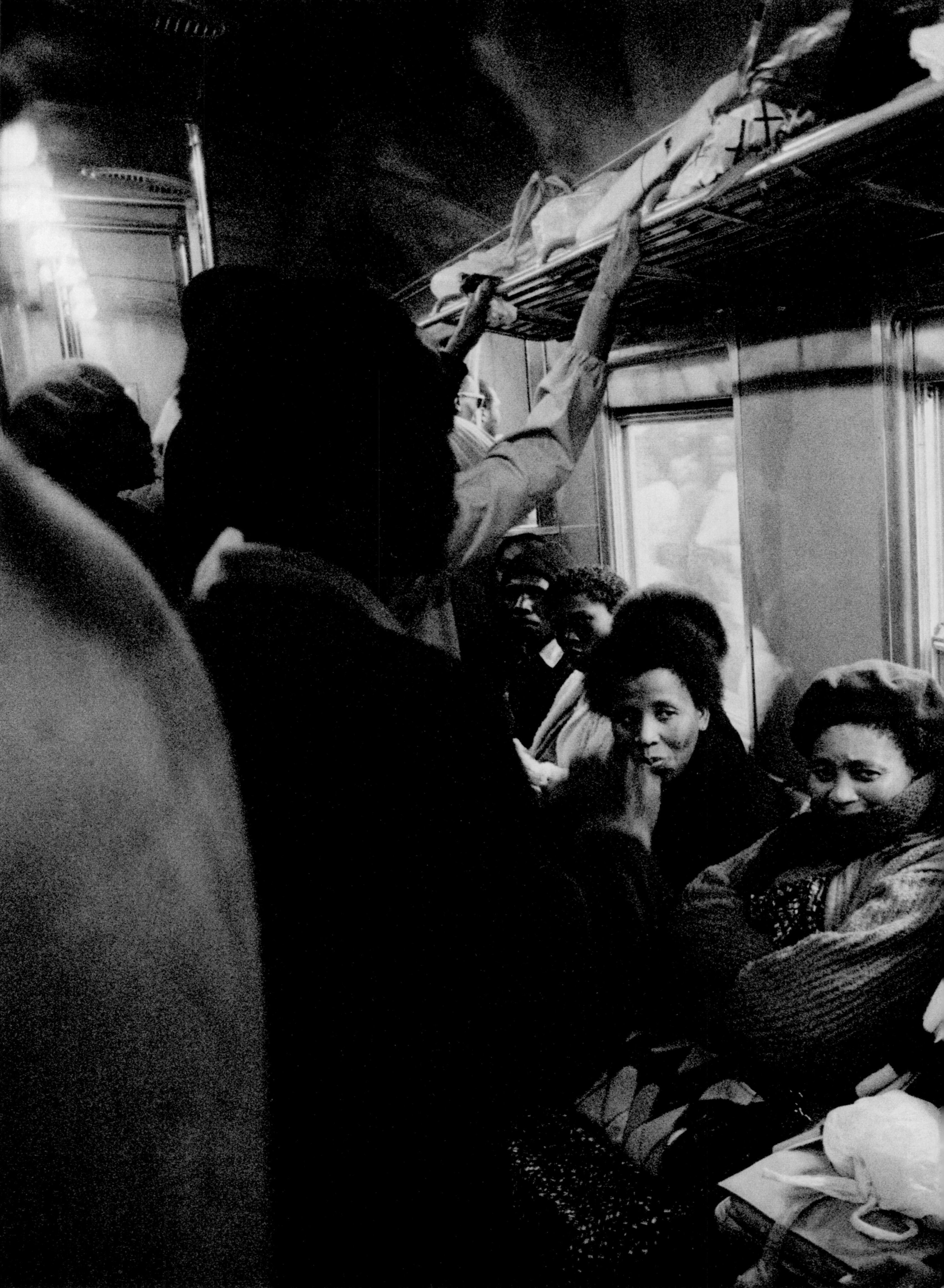

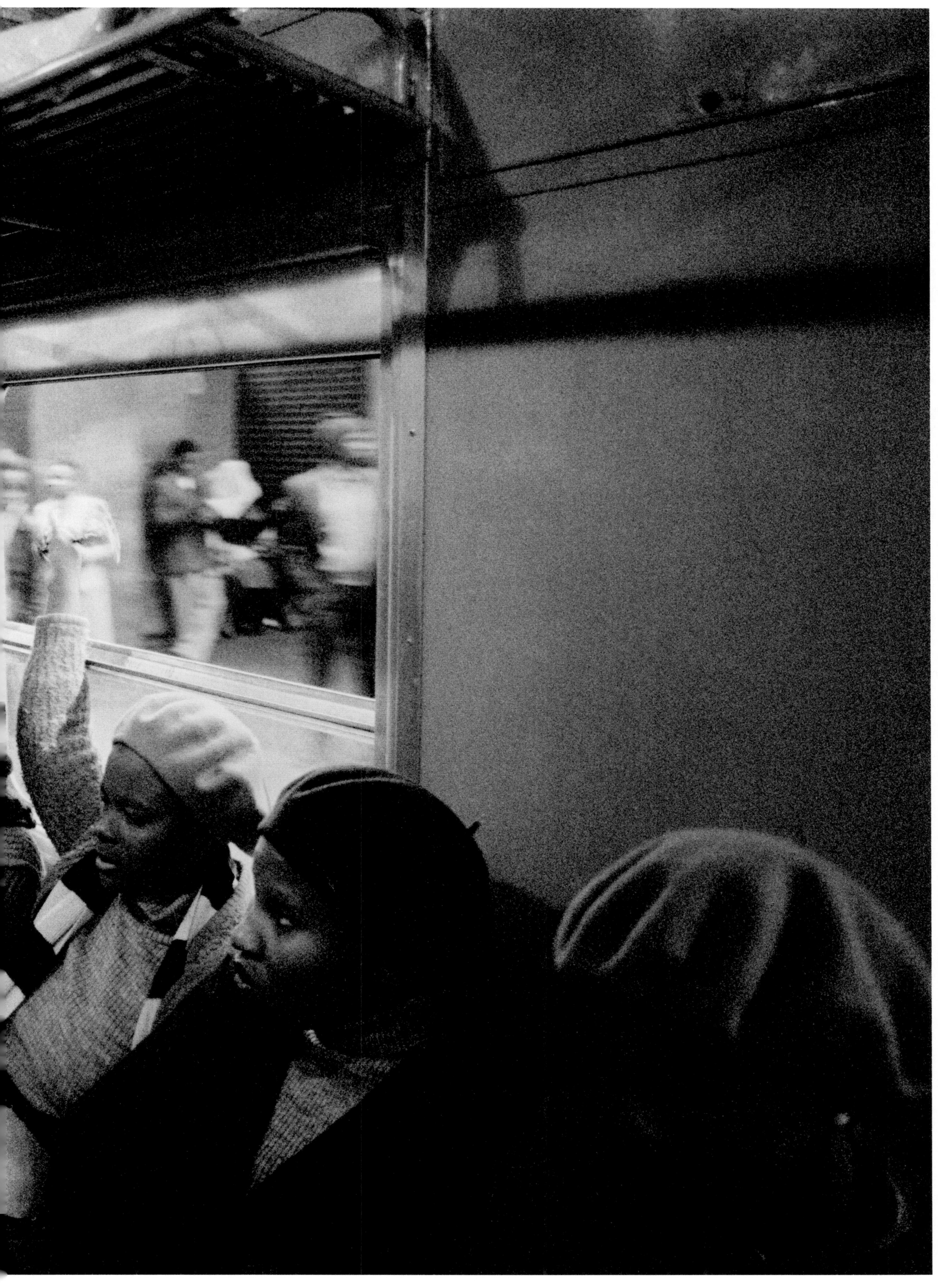

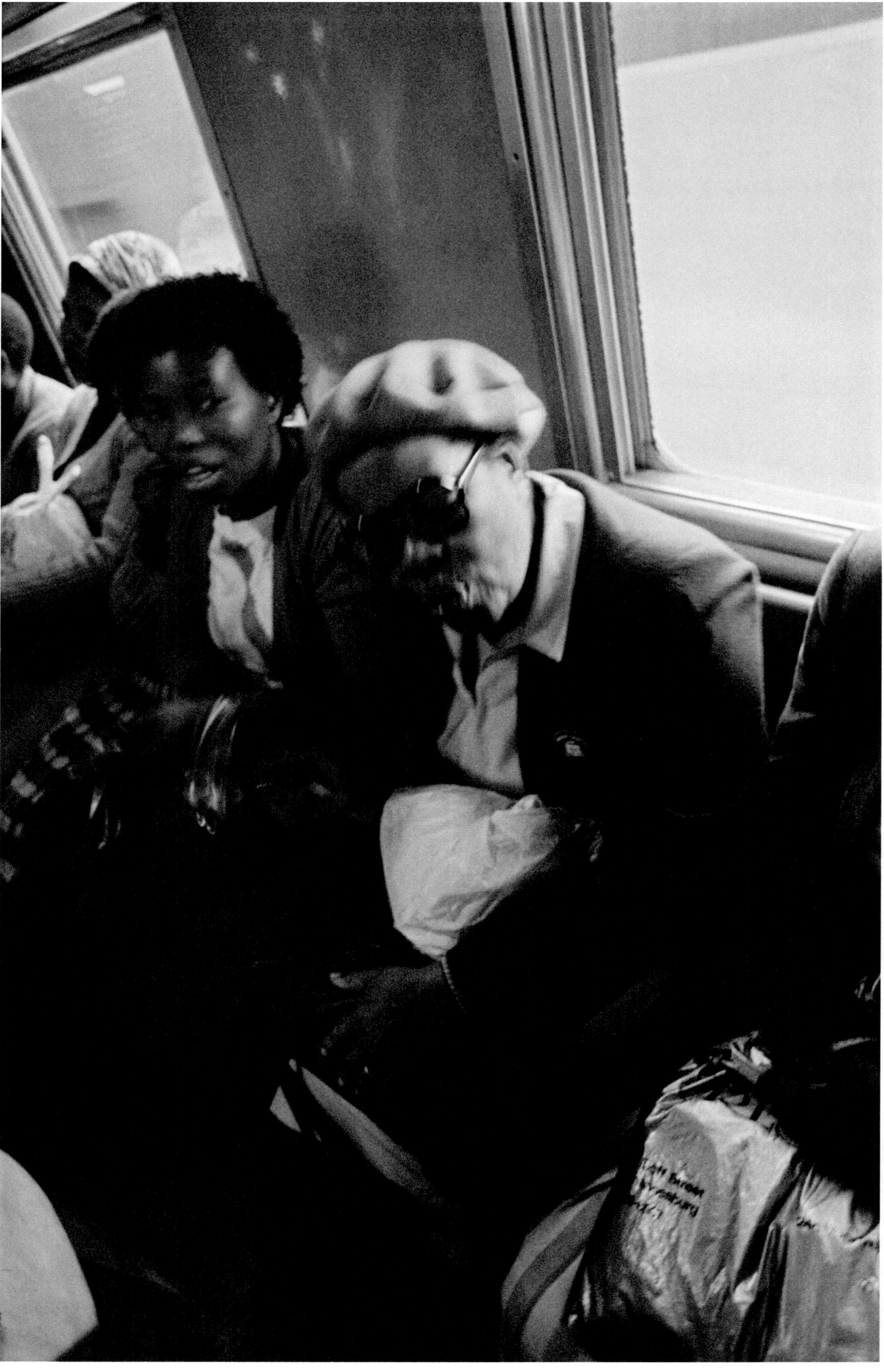

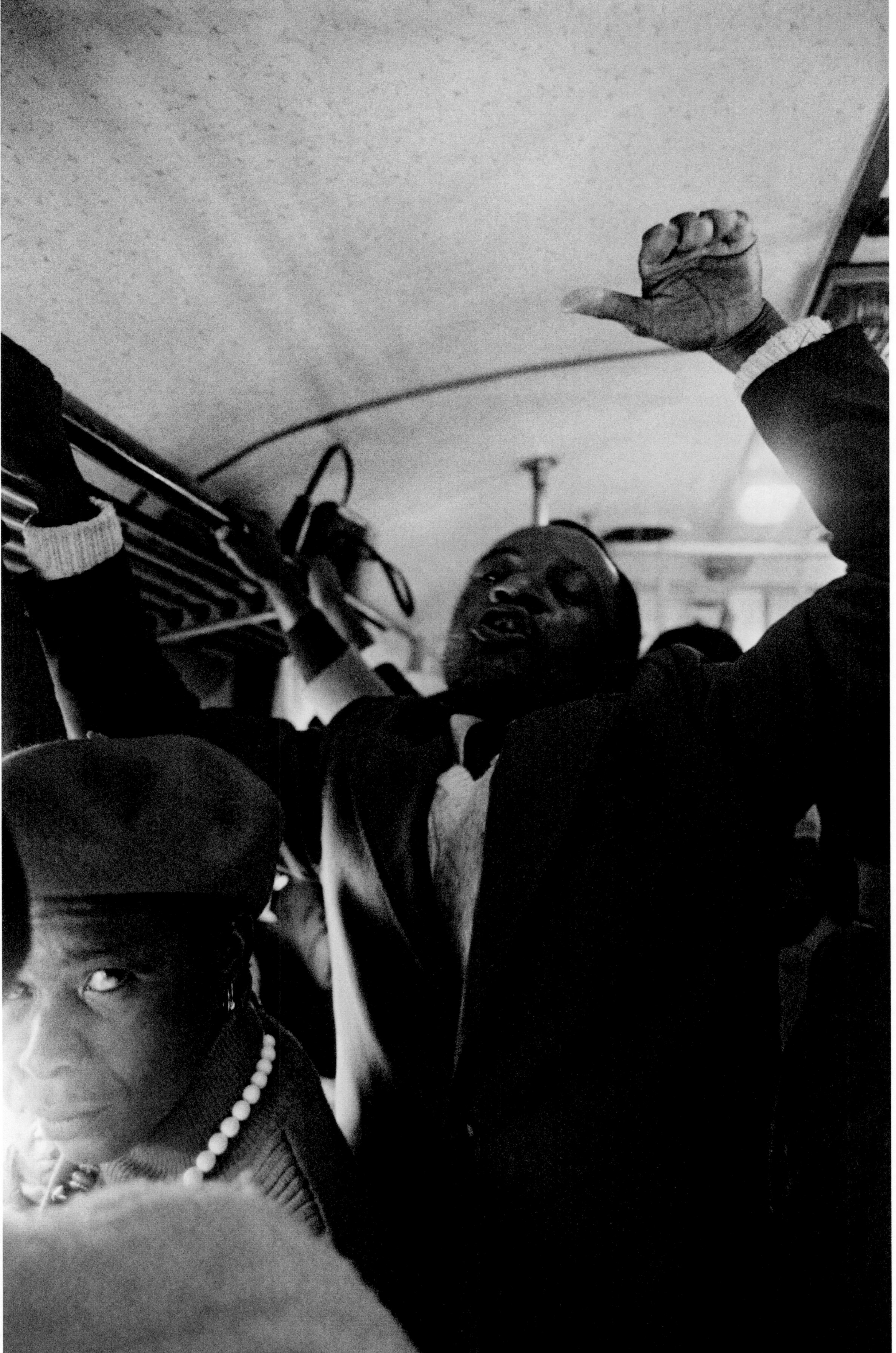

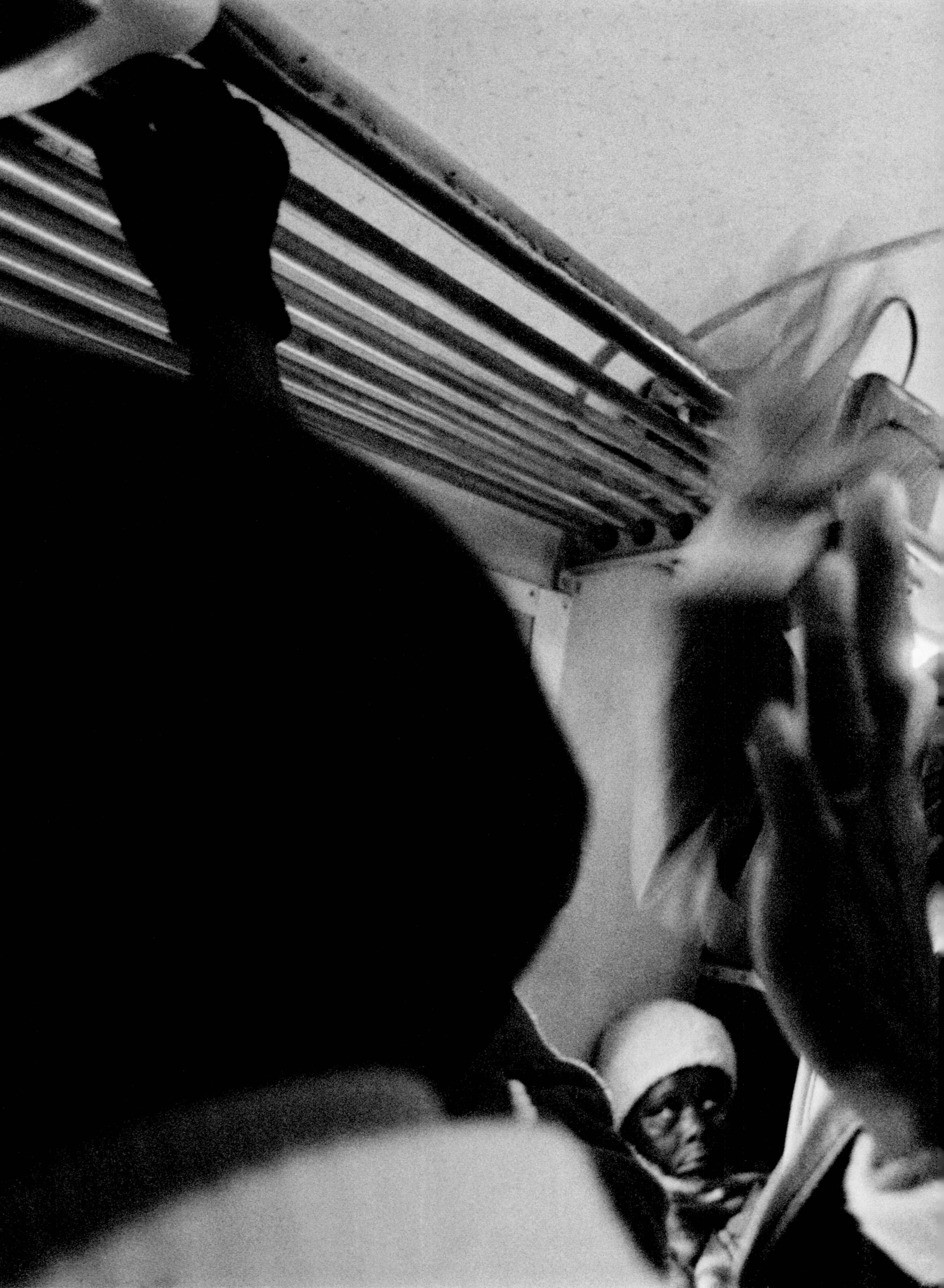

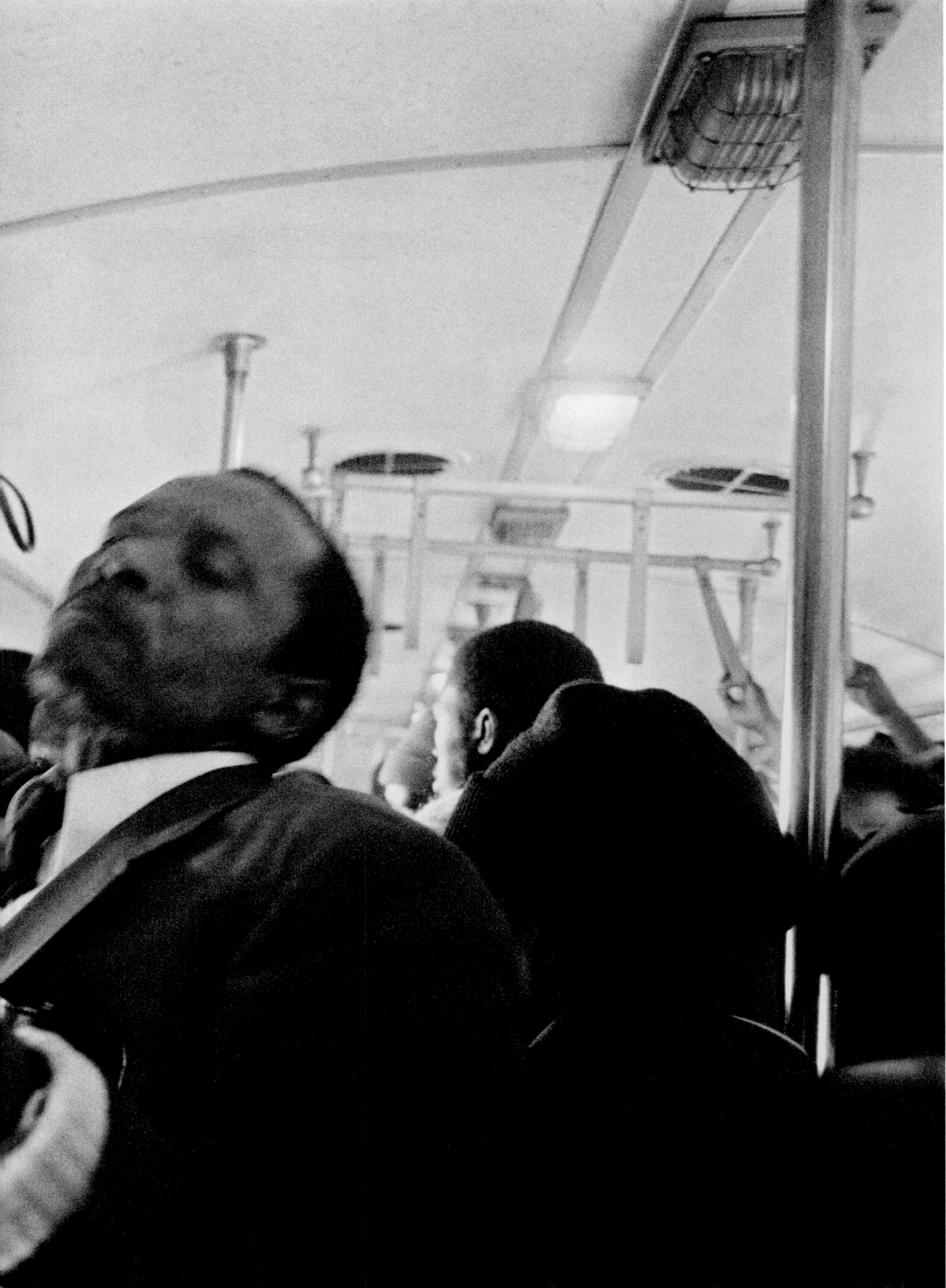

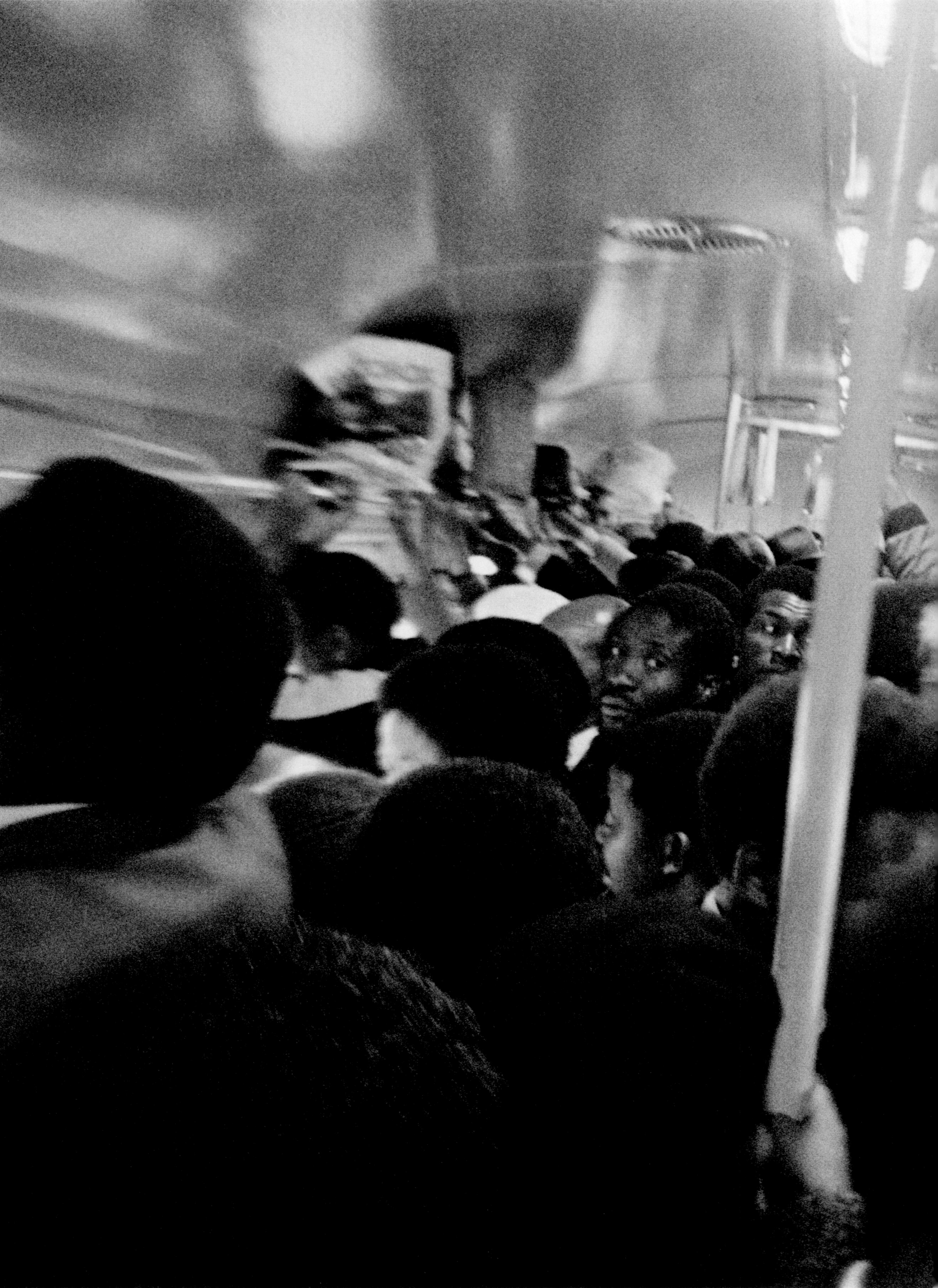

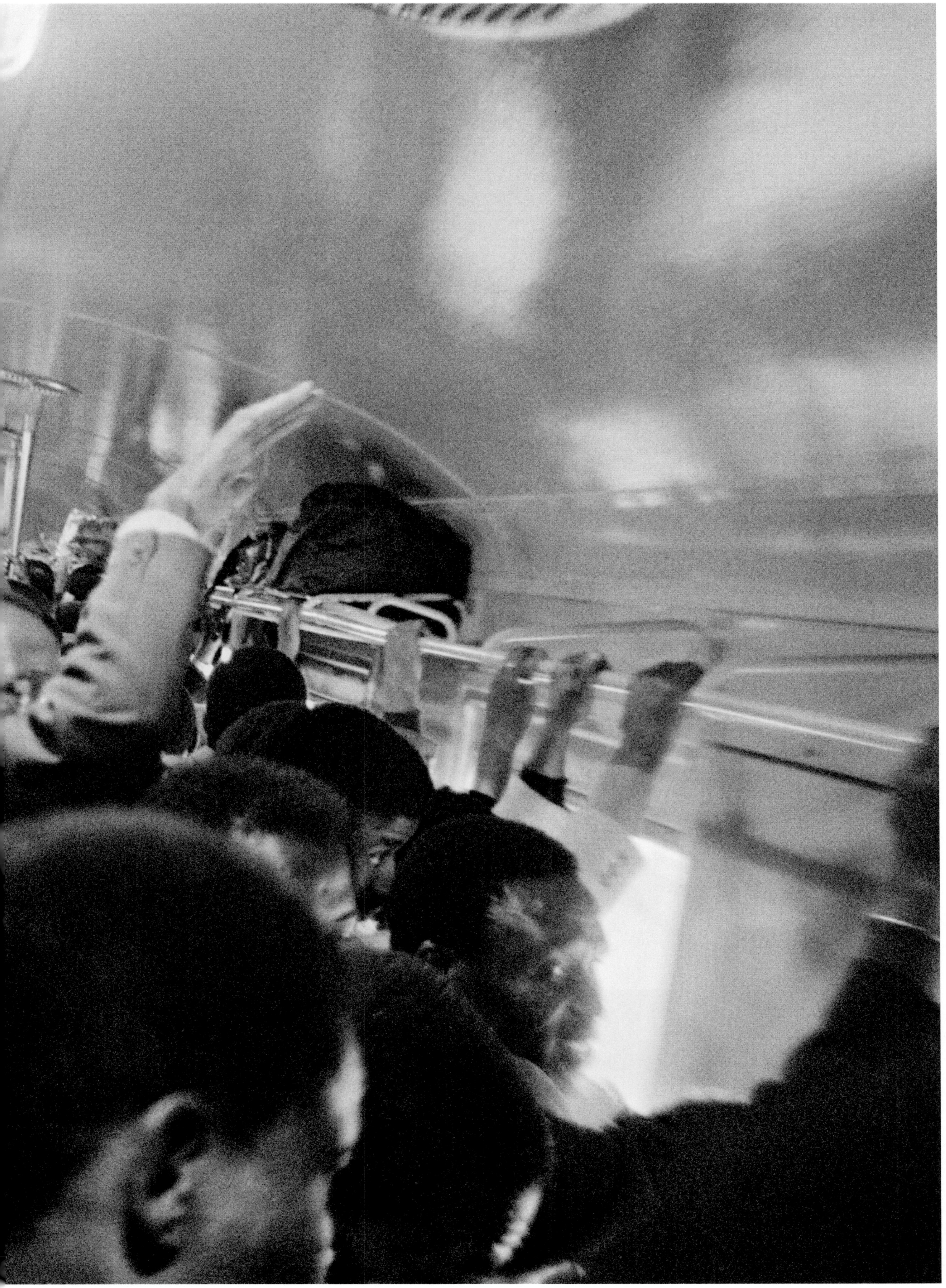

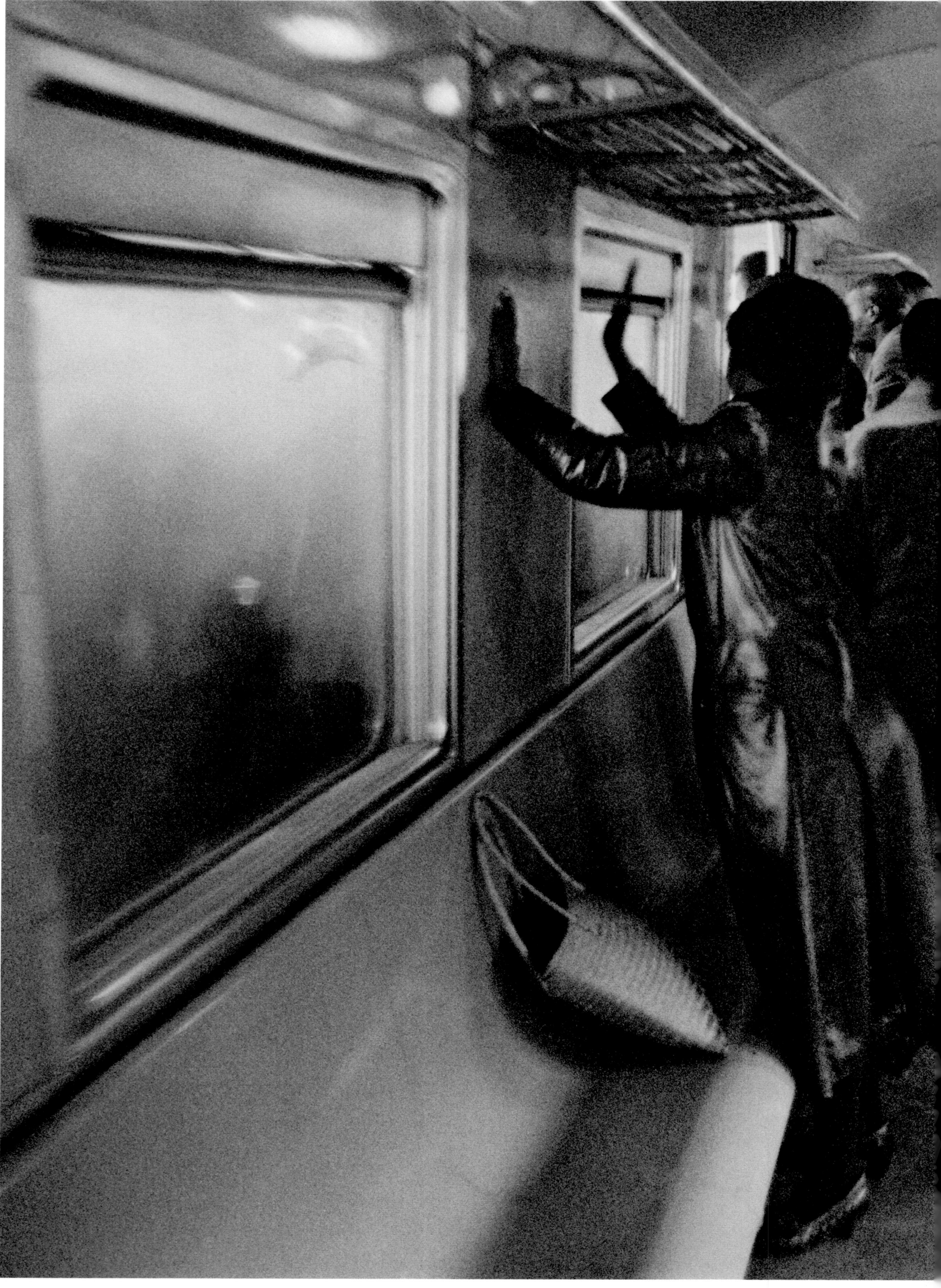

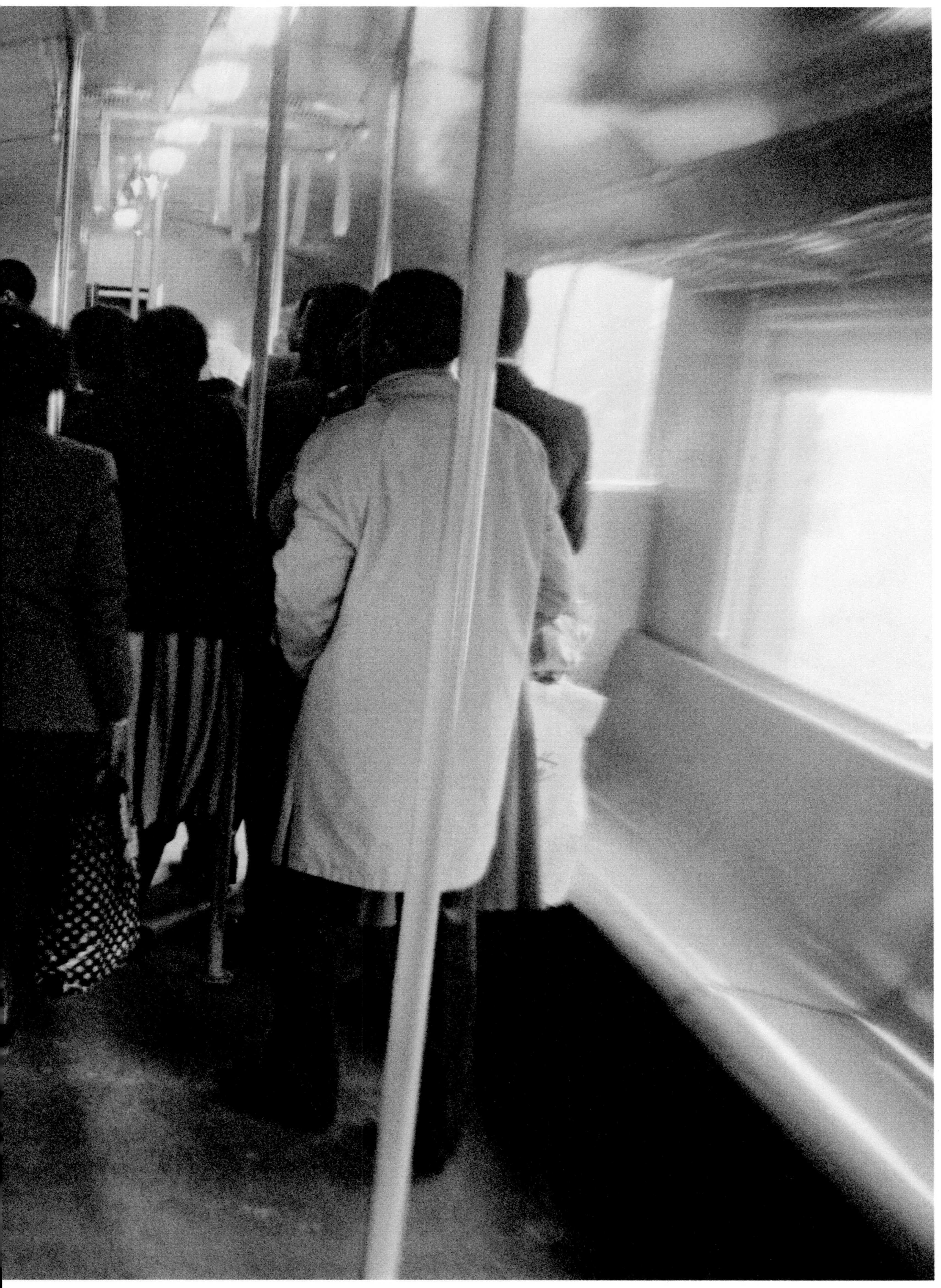

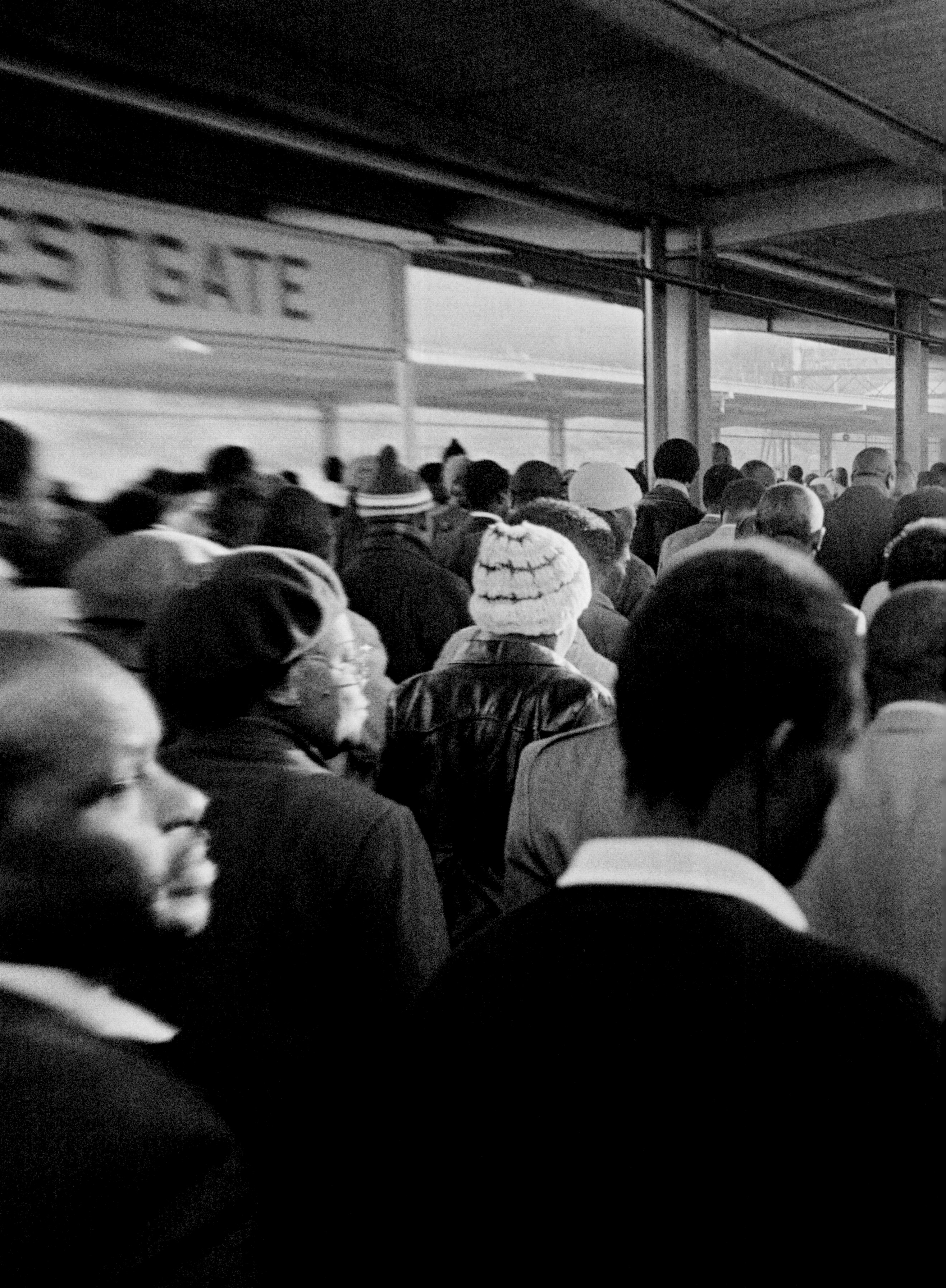
EST GATE

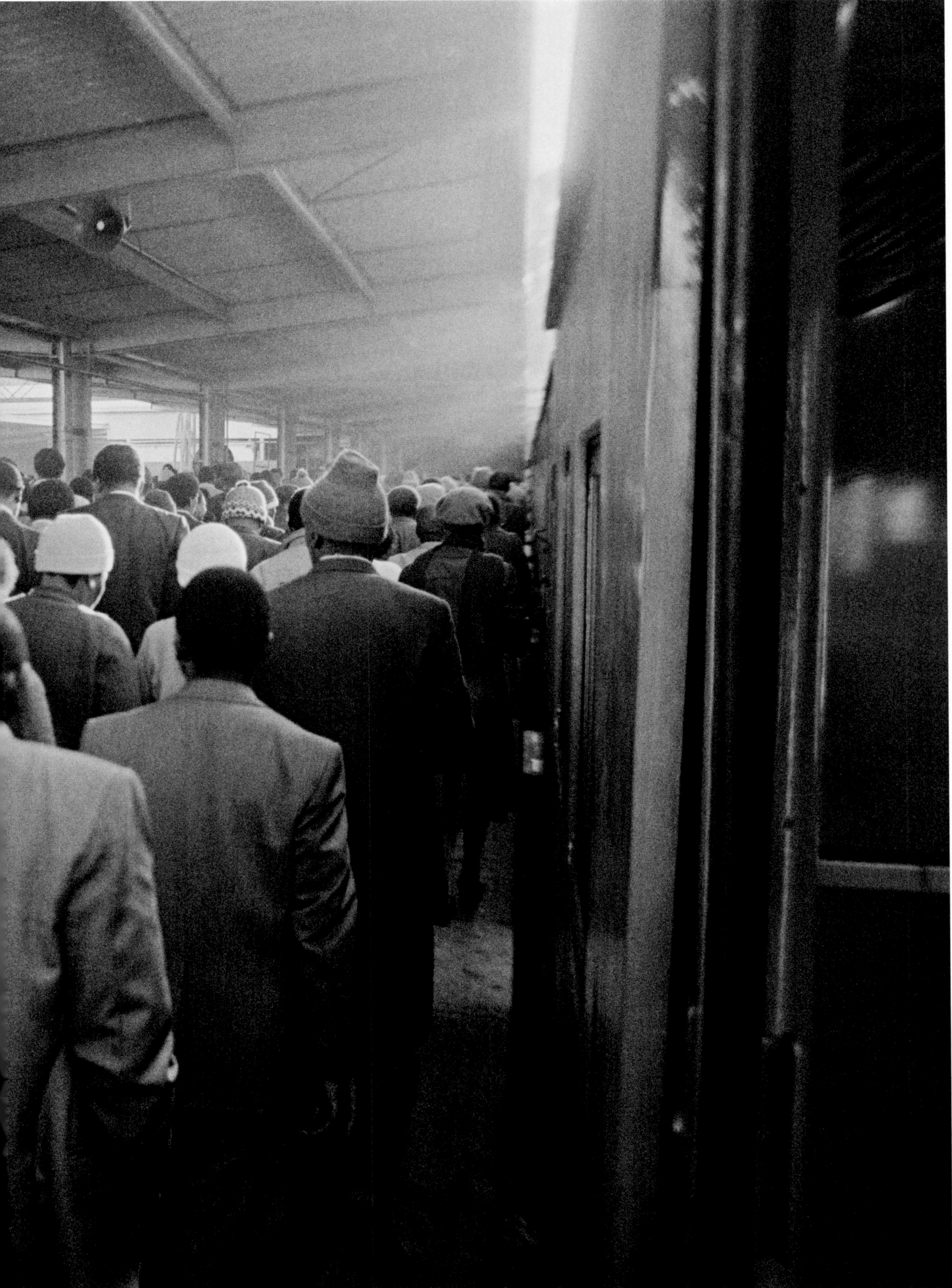

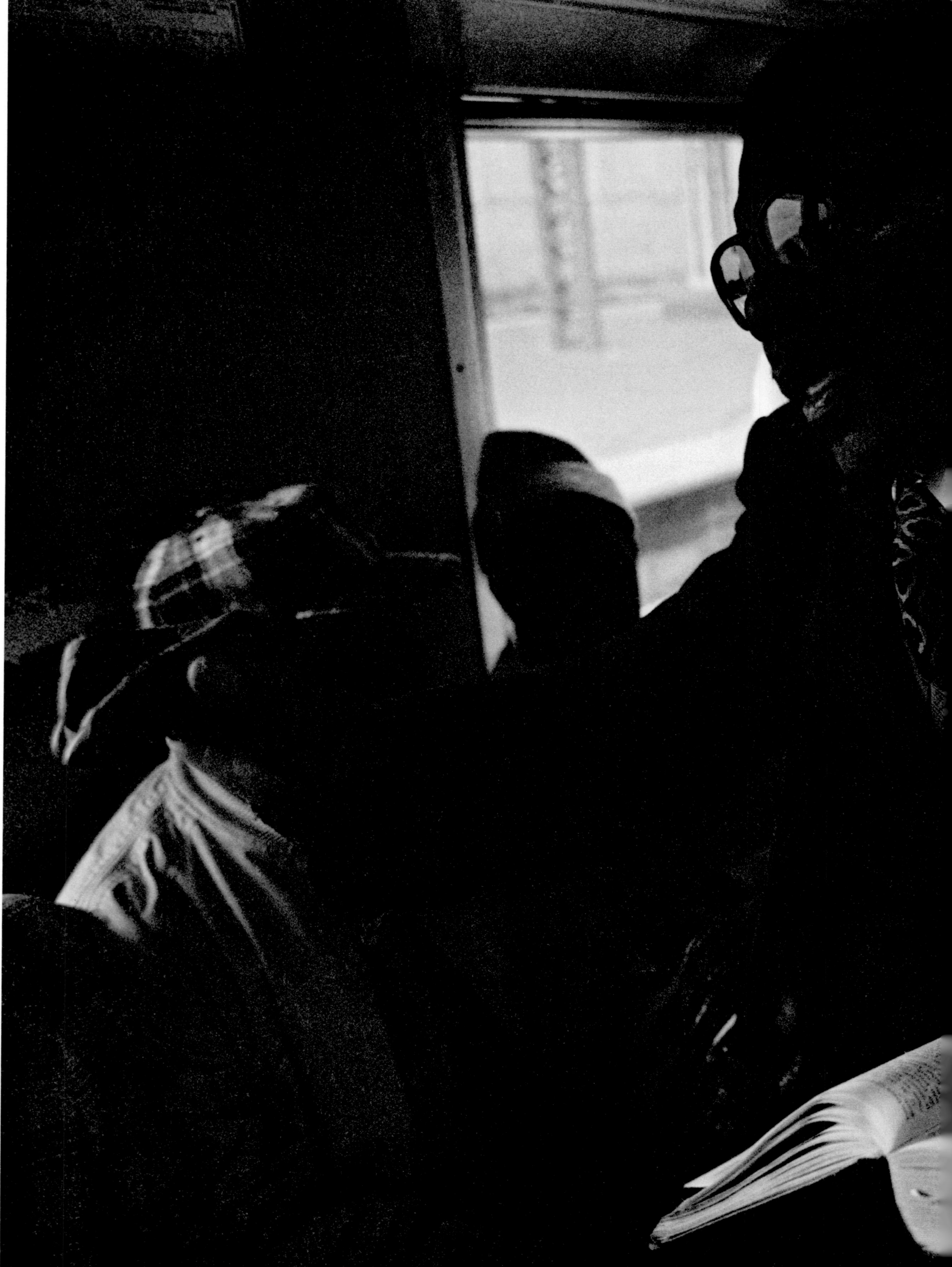

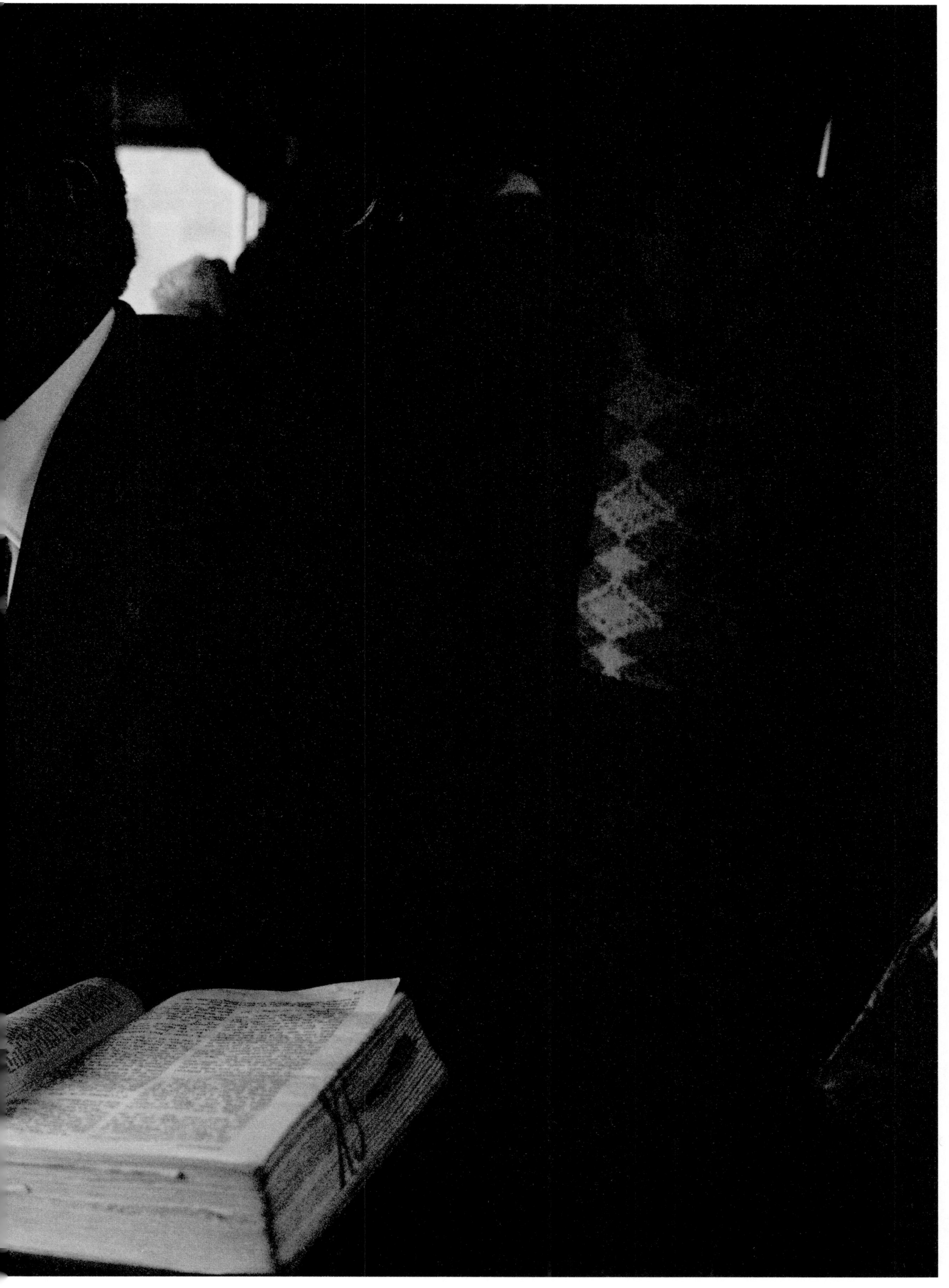

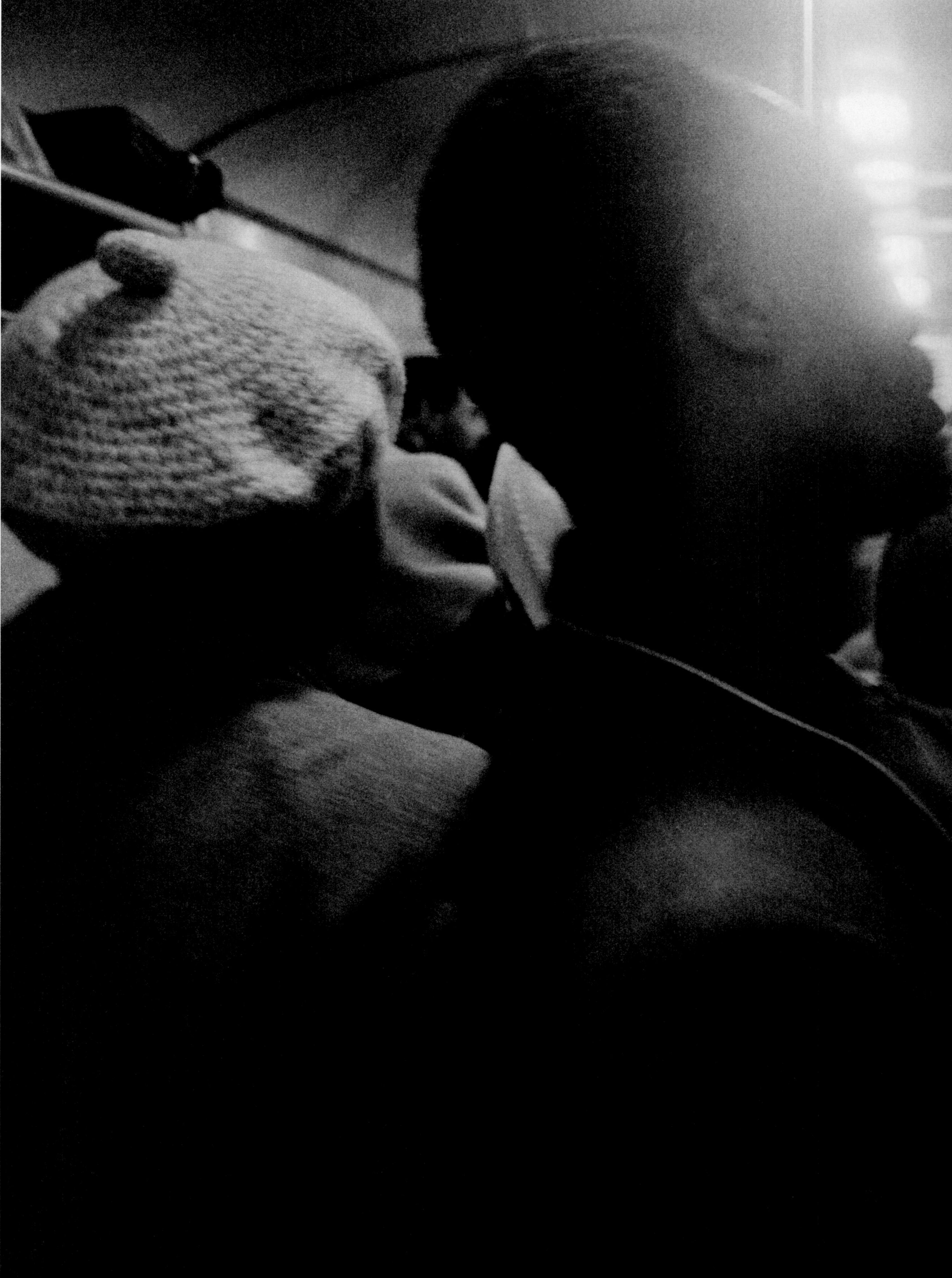

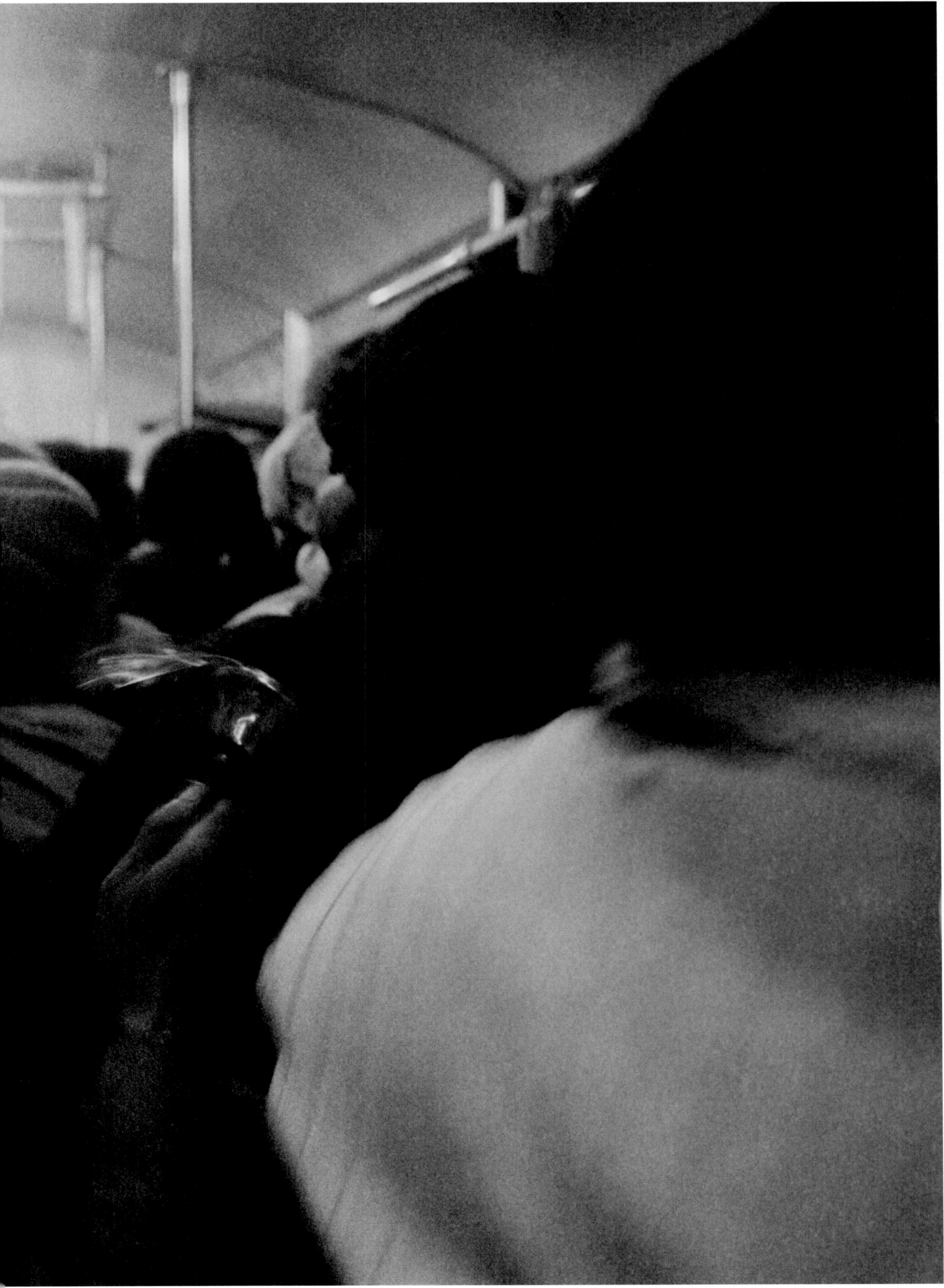

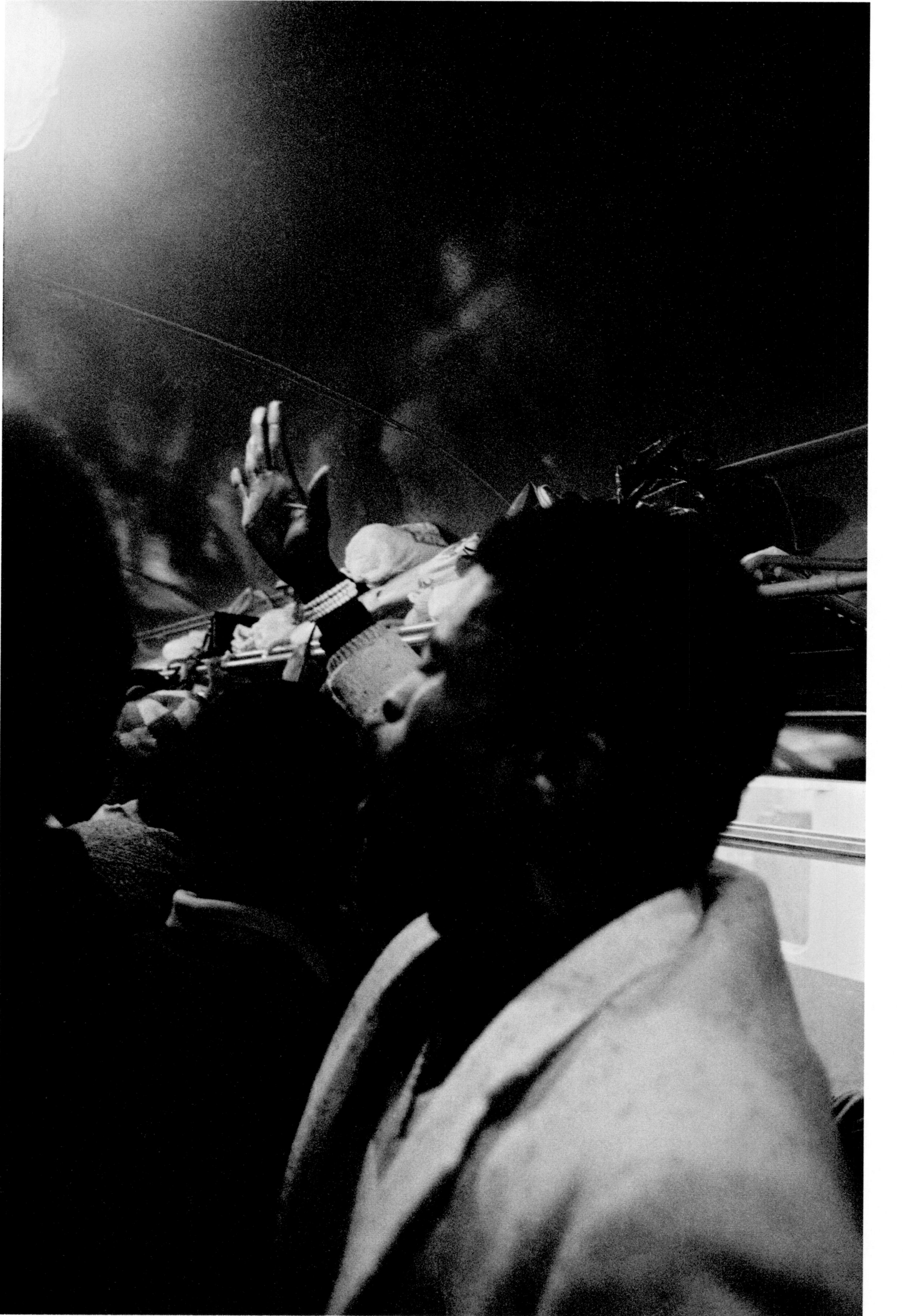

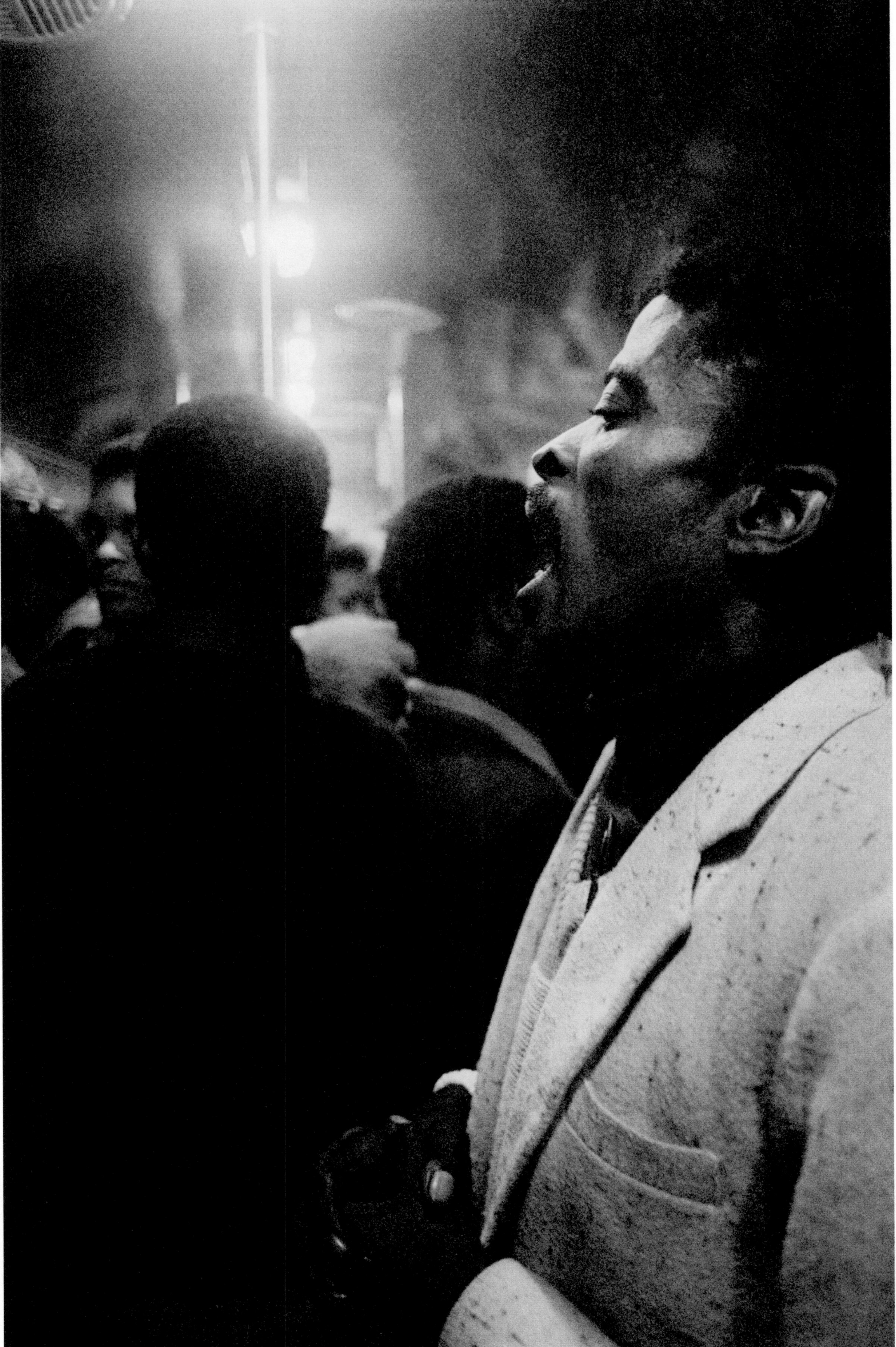

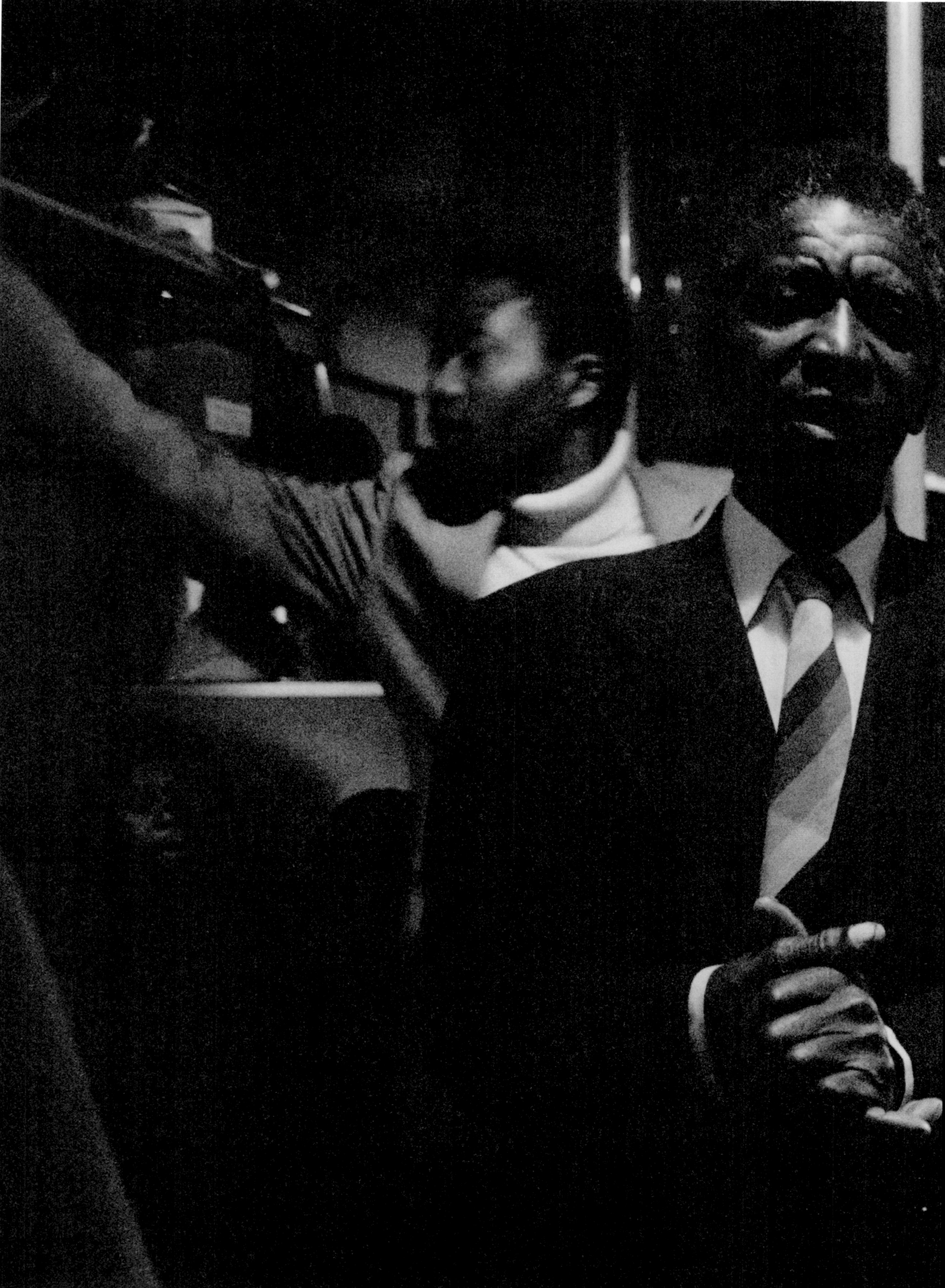

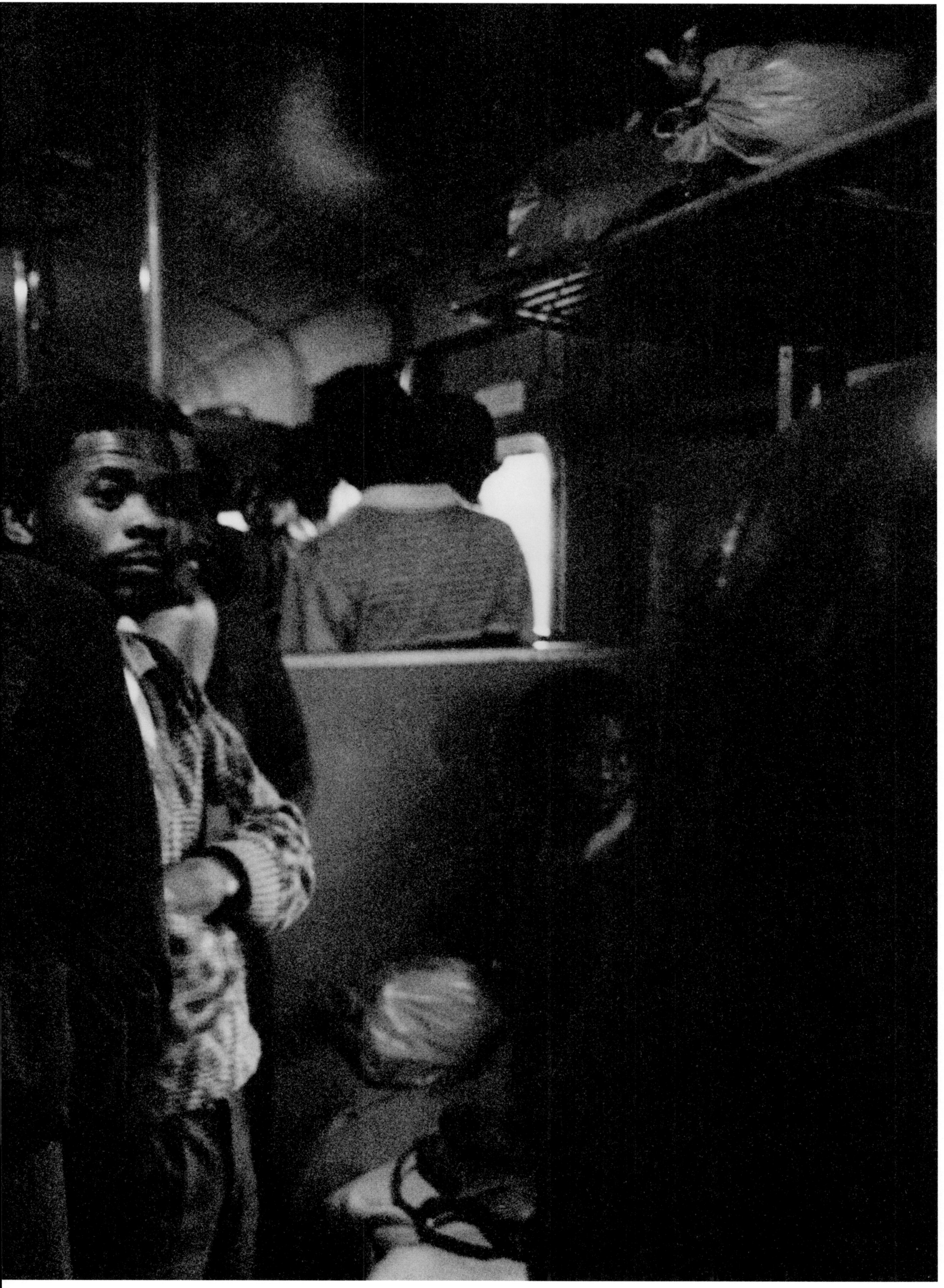

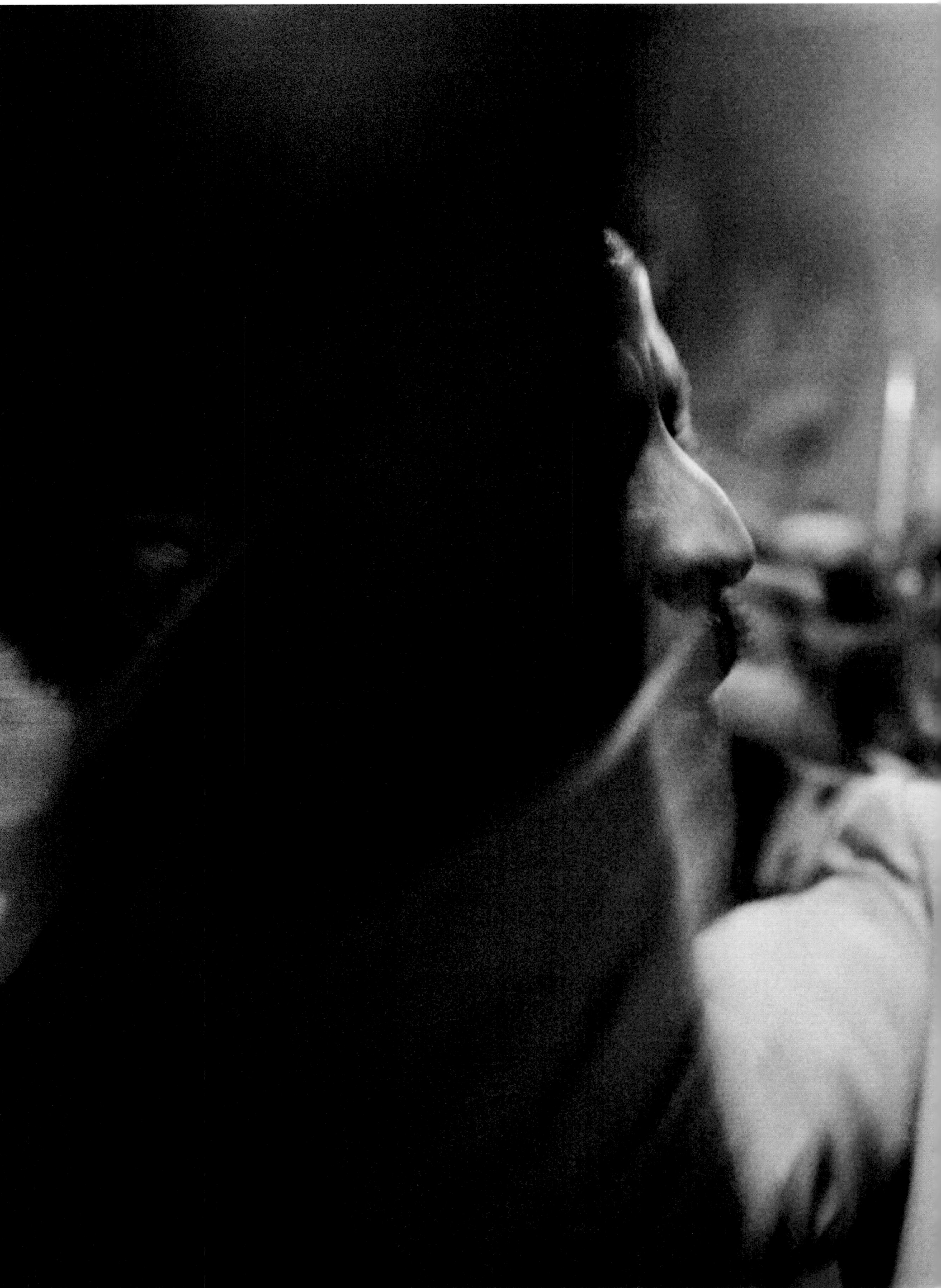

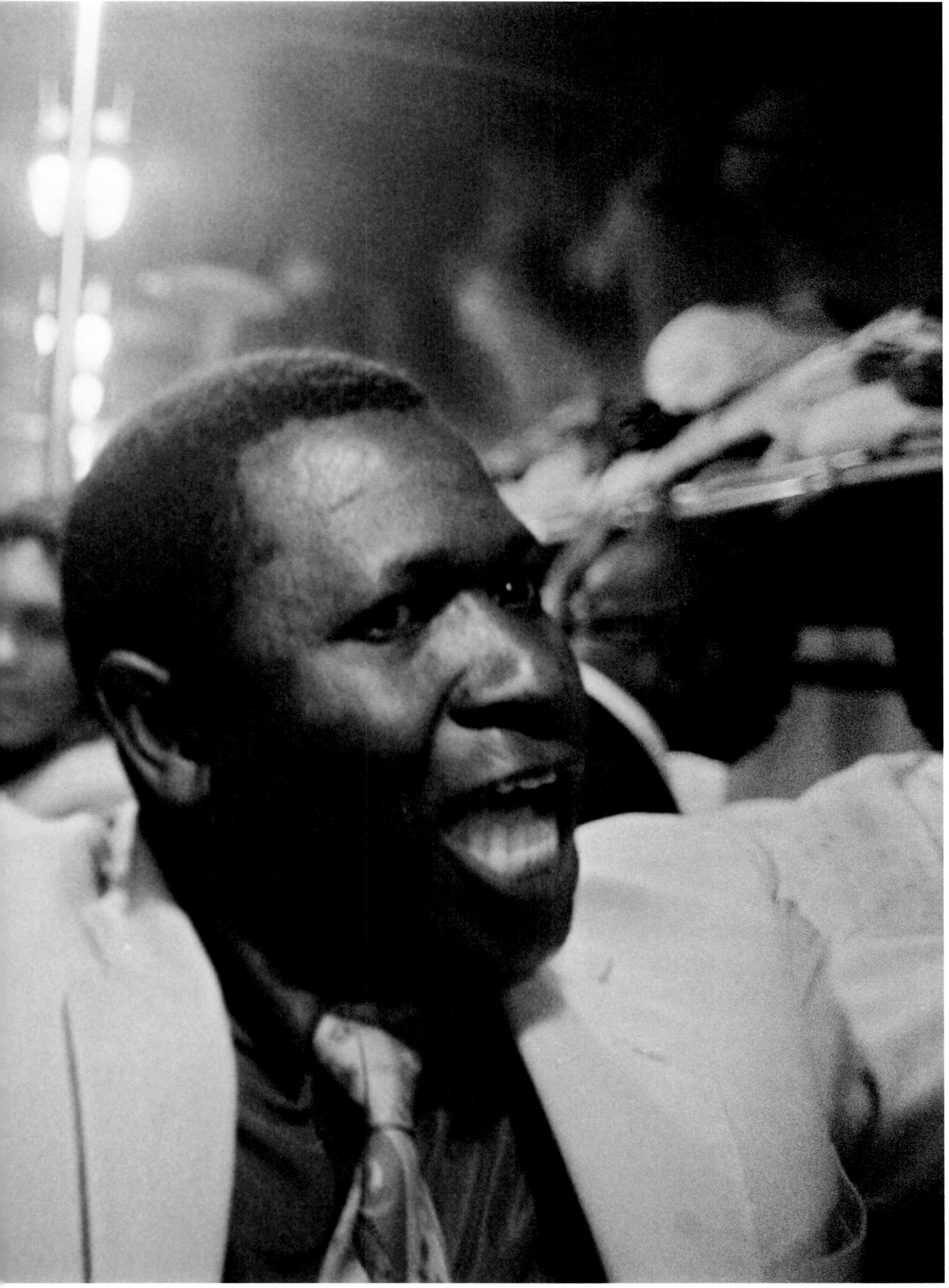

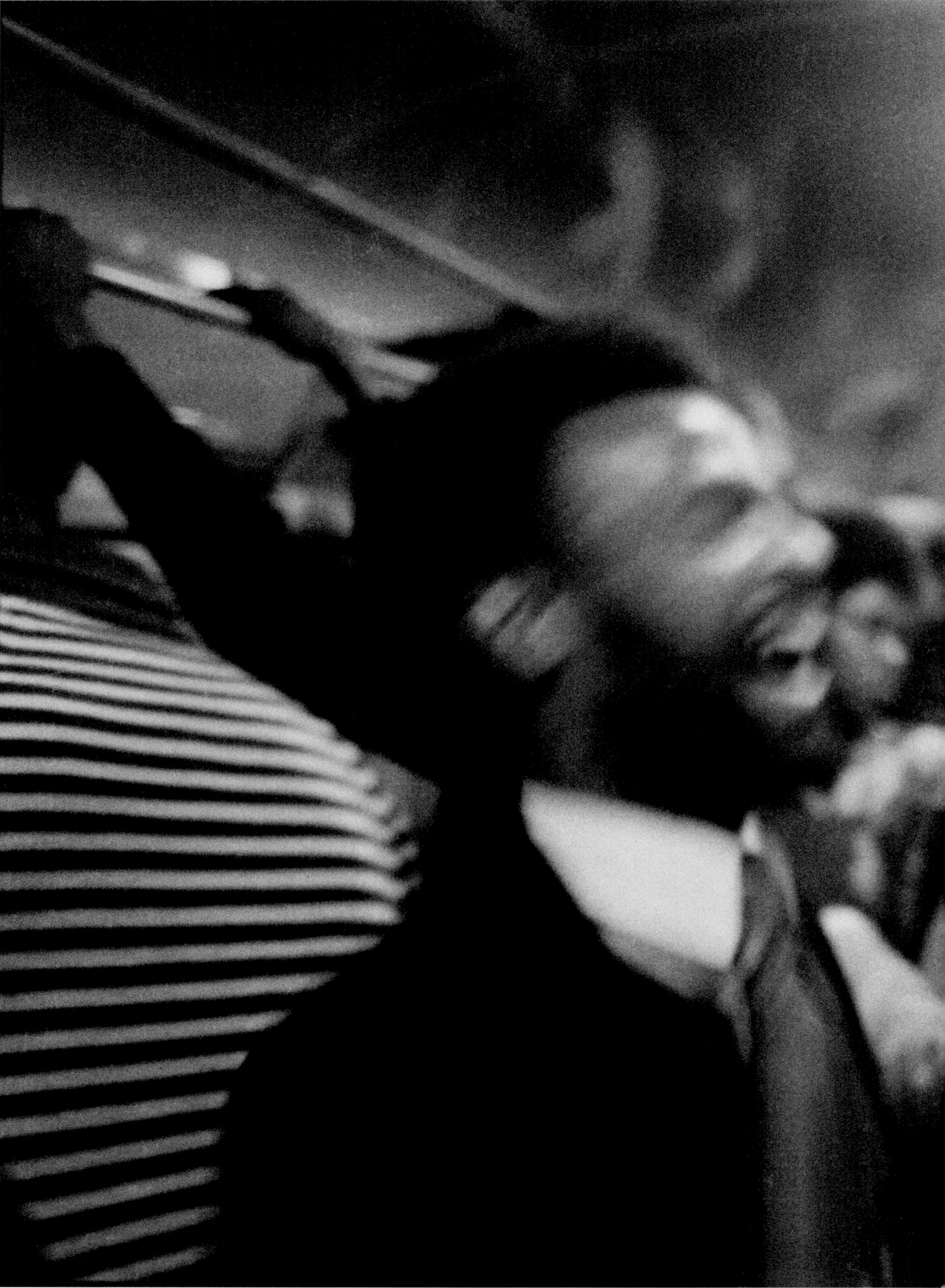

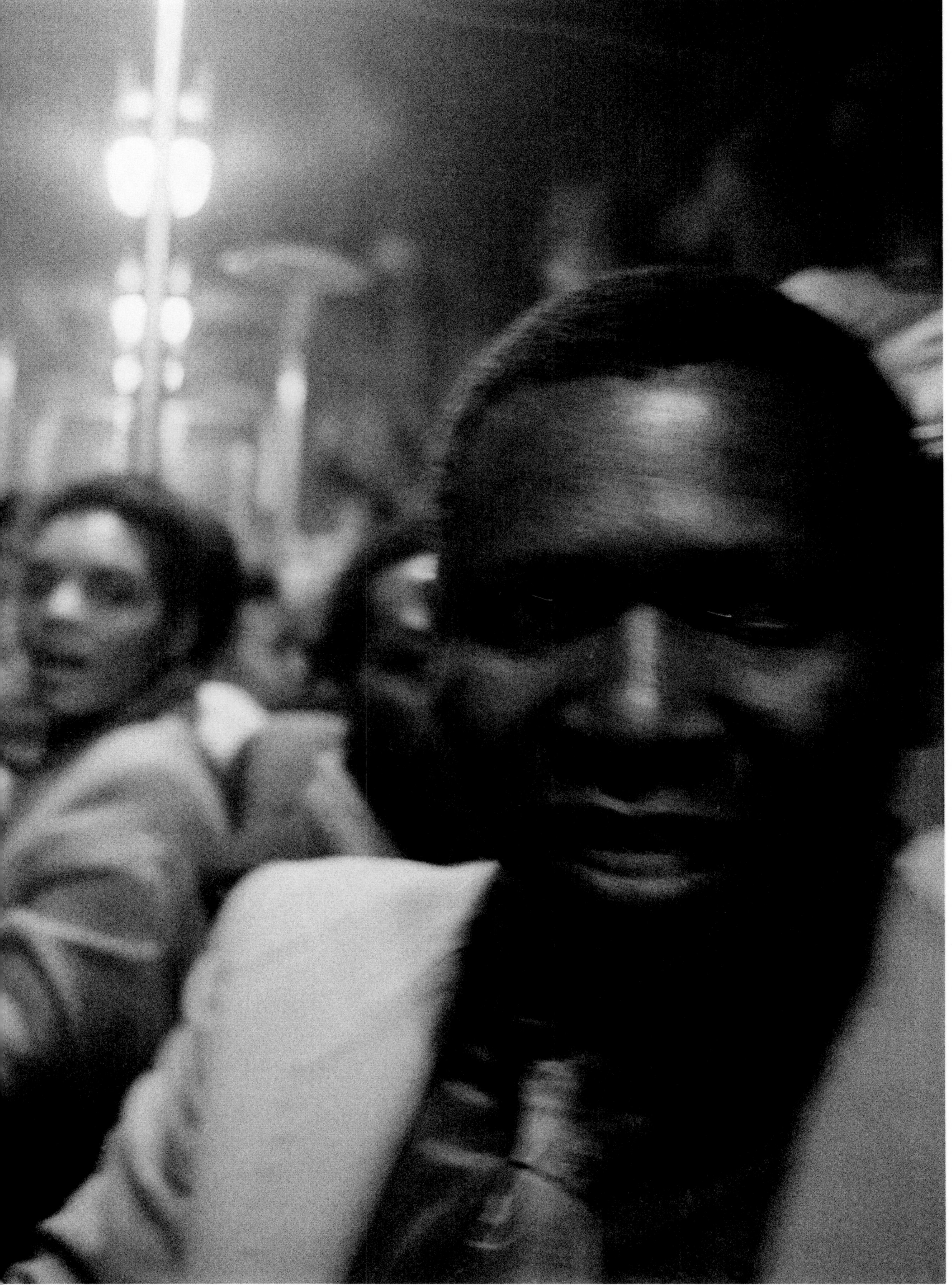

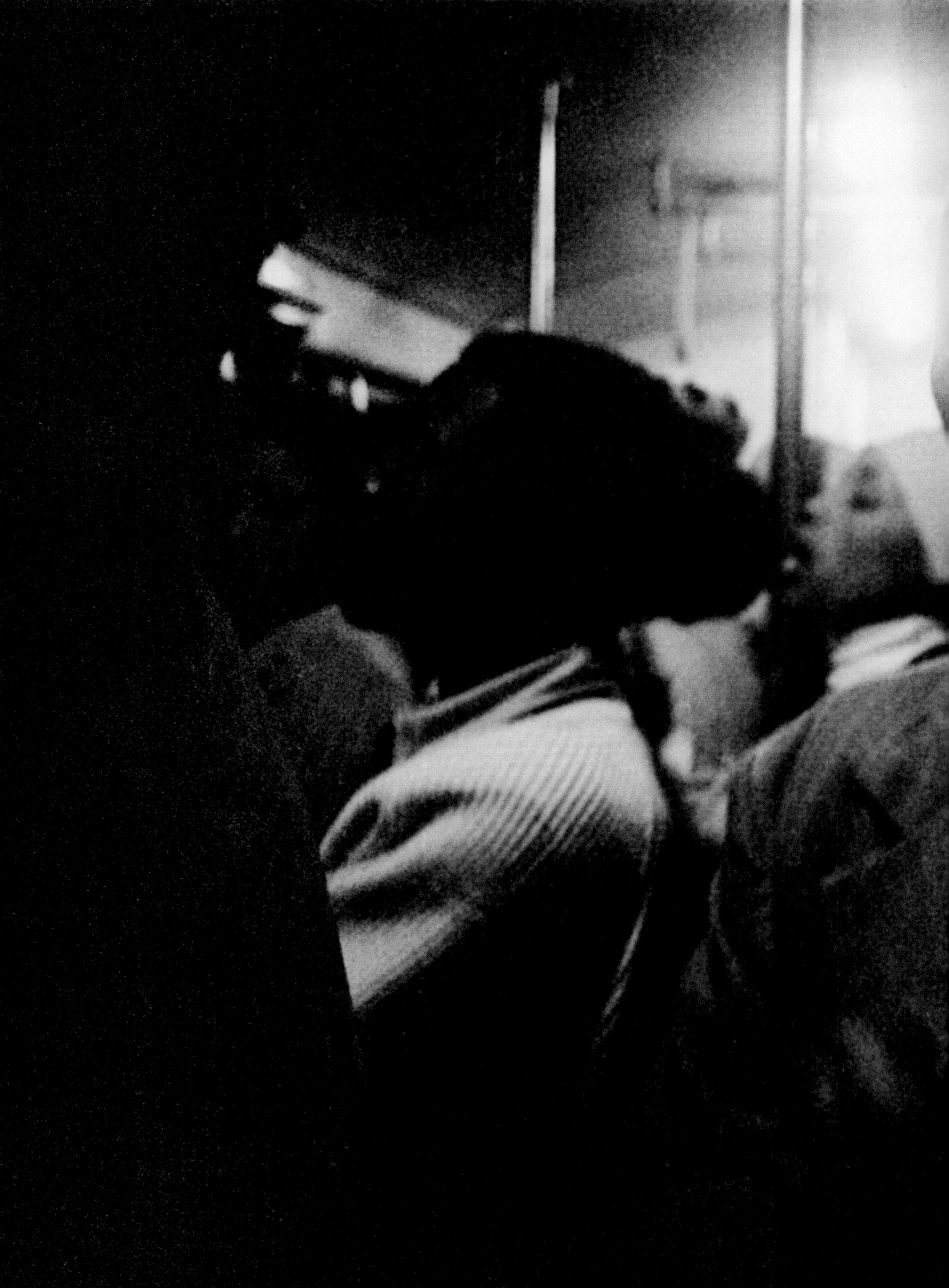

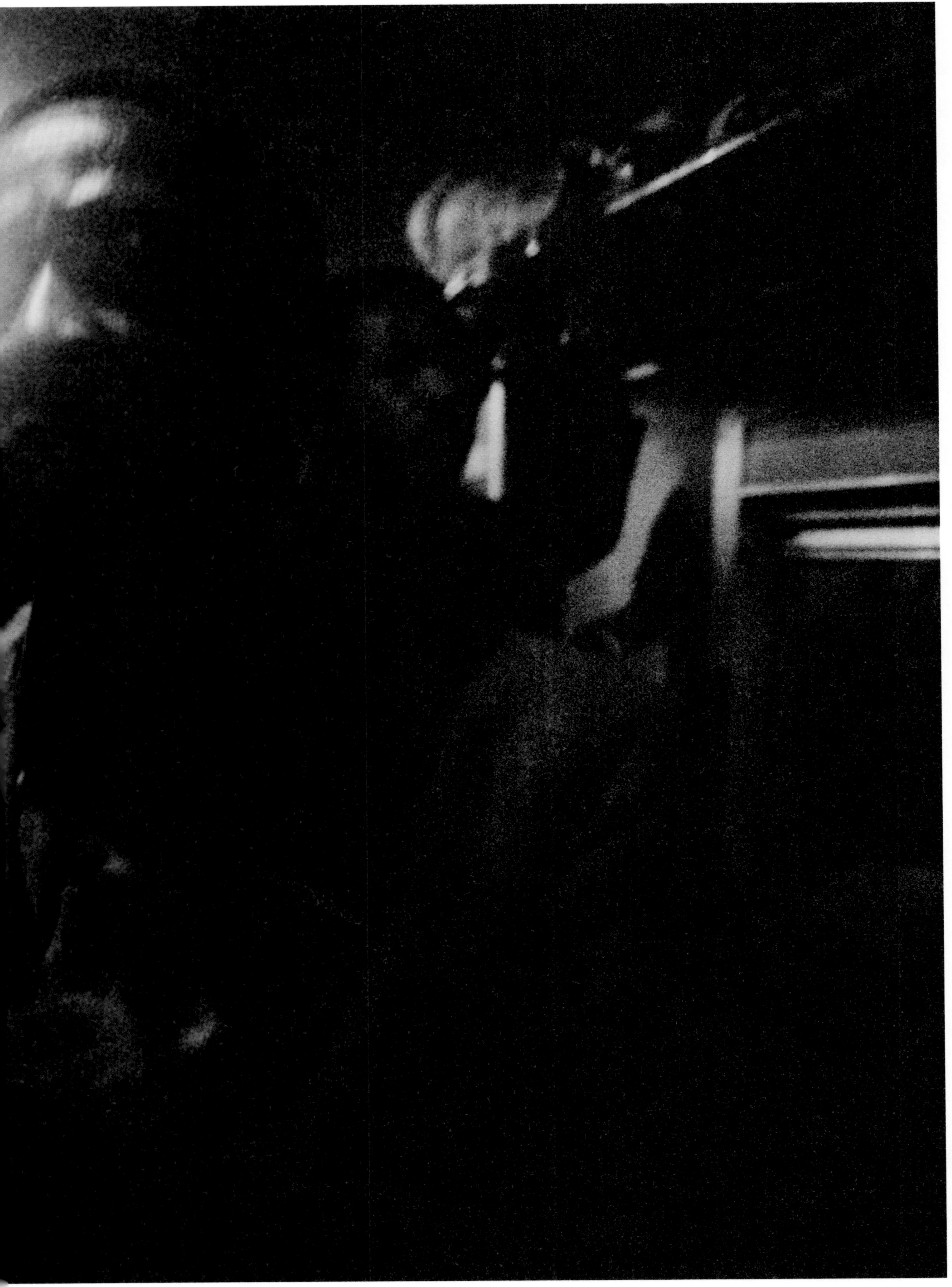

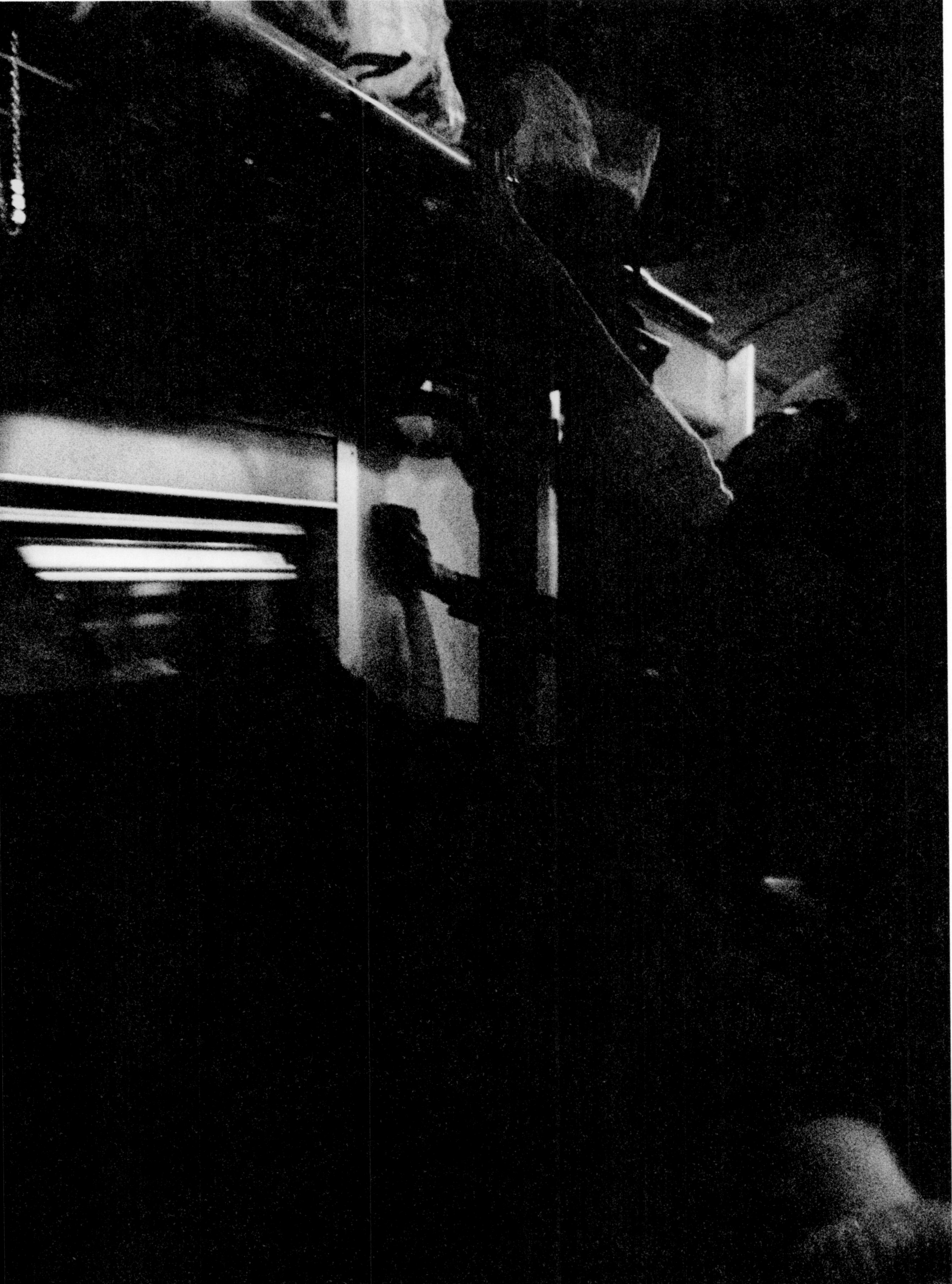

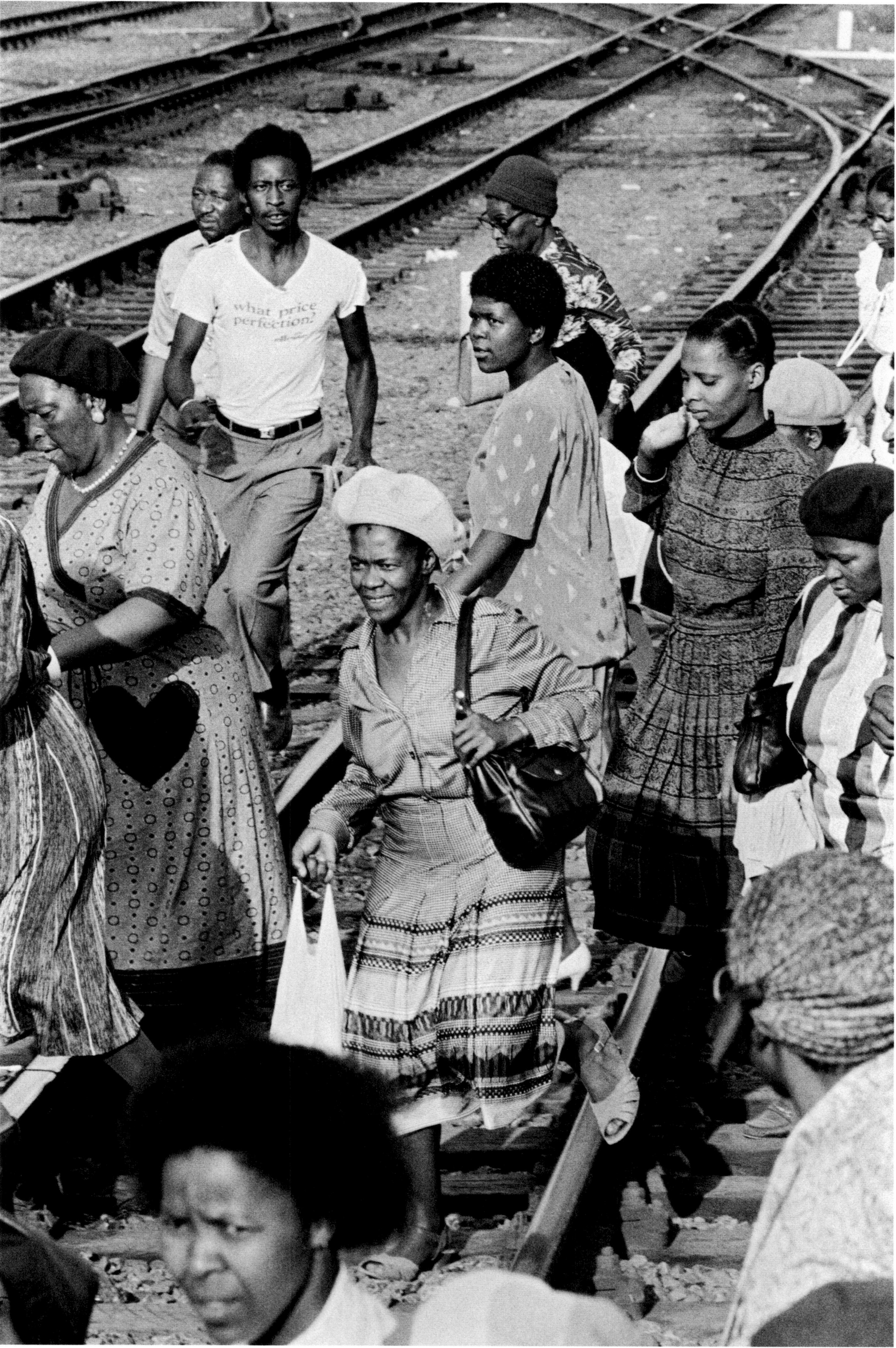

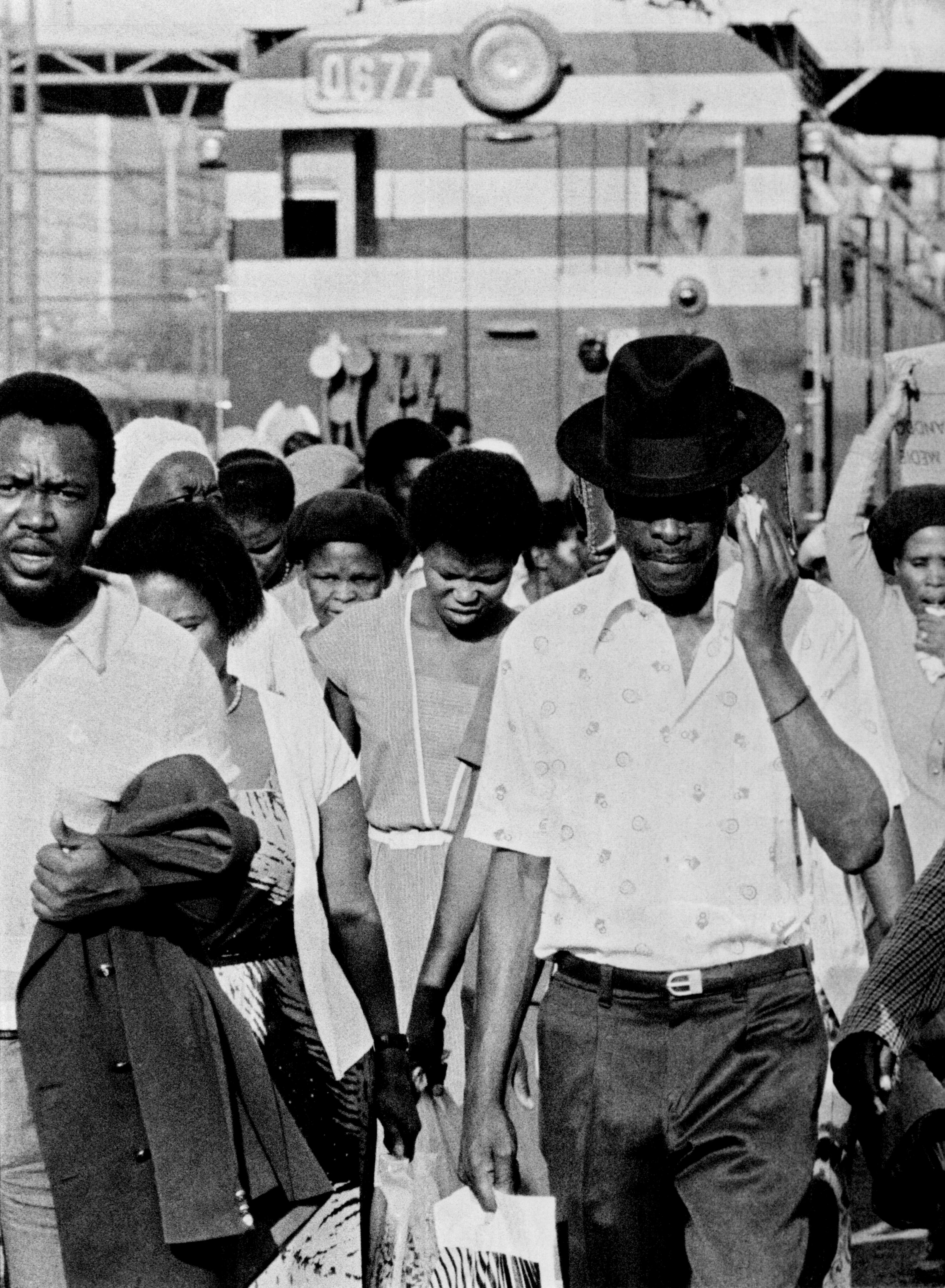

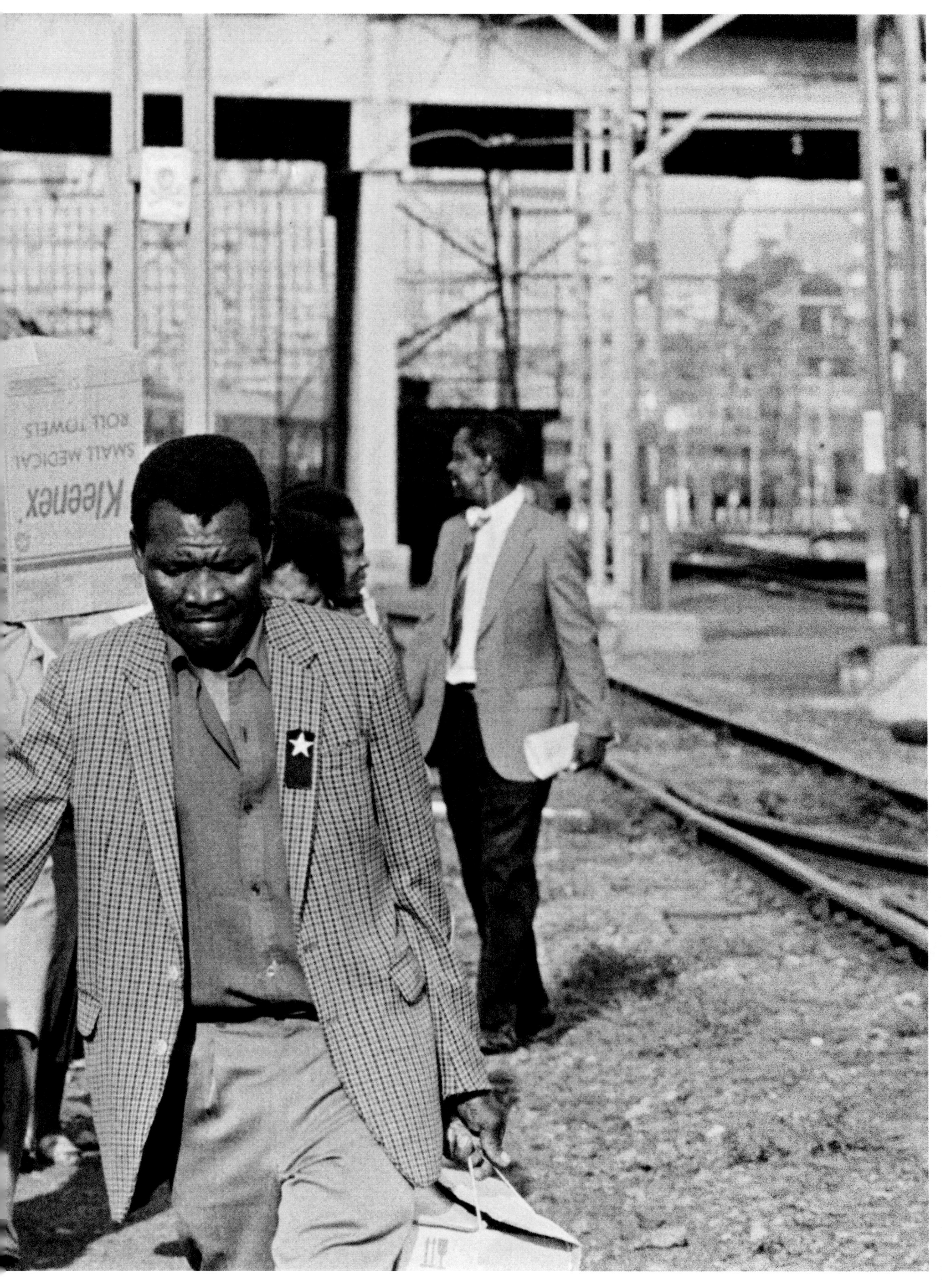
Kleenex*
SMALL MEDICAL ROLL TOWELS

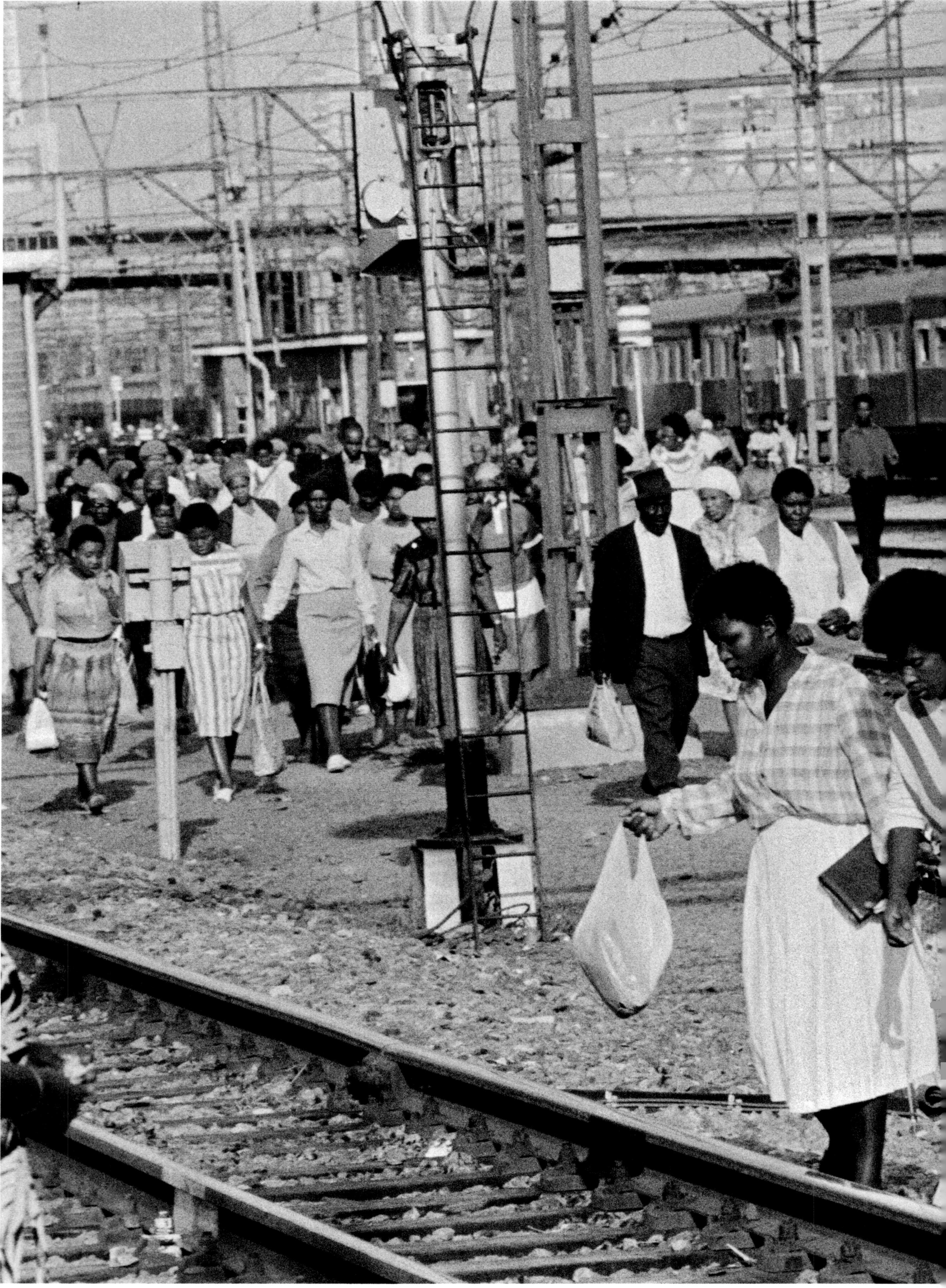

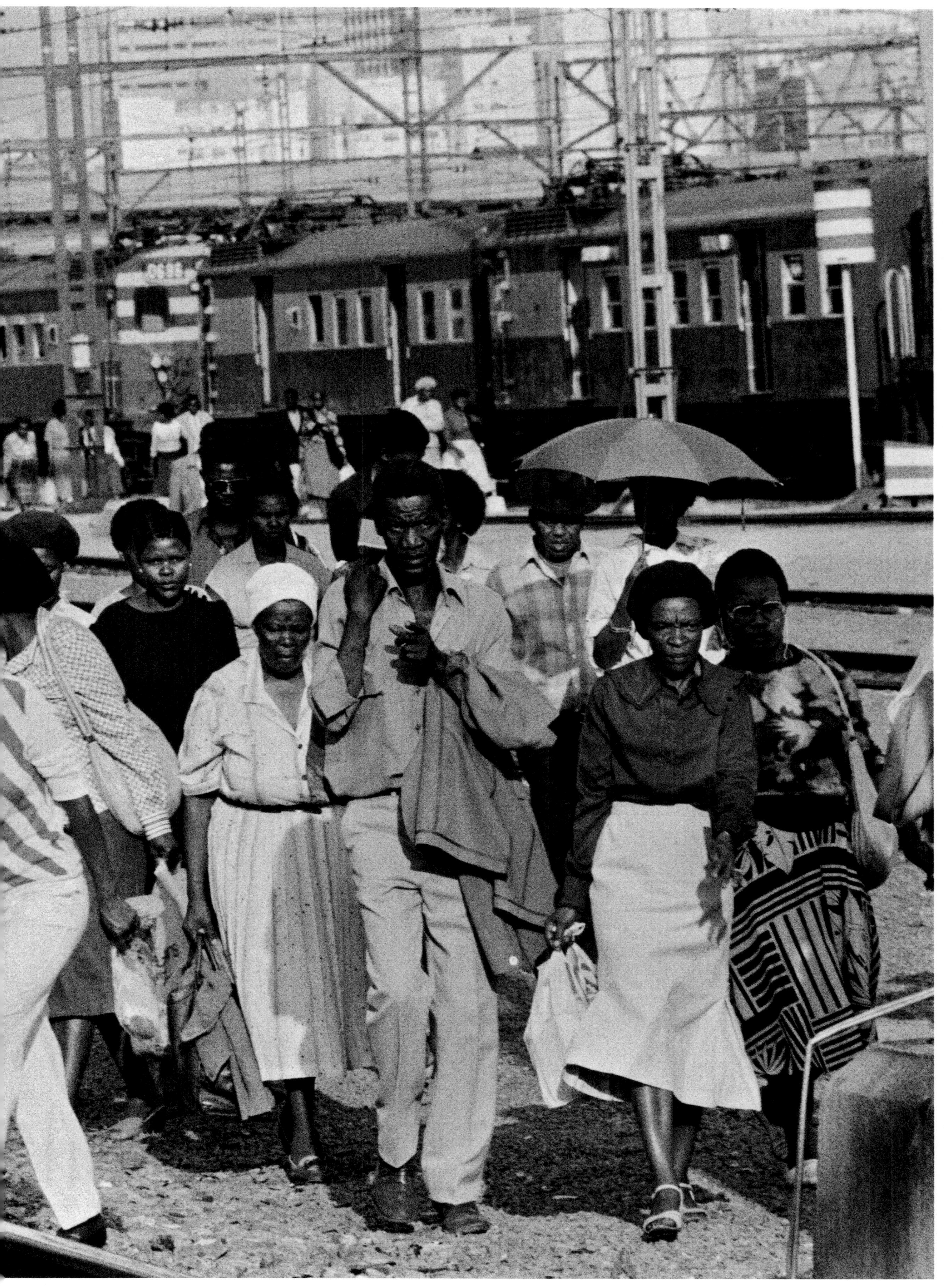

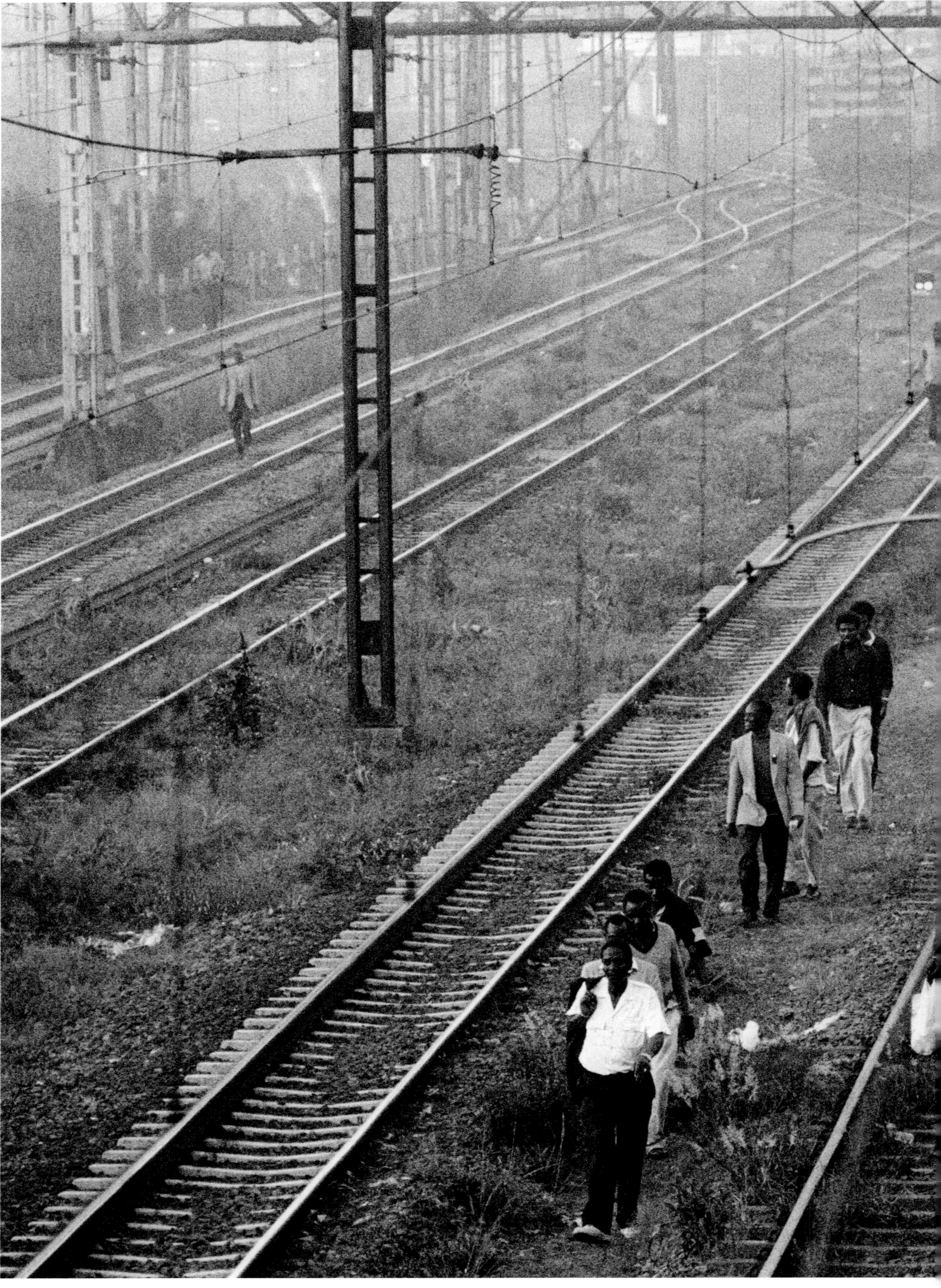

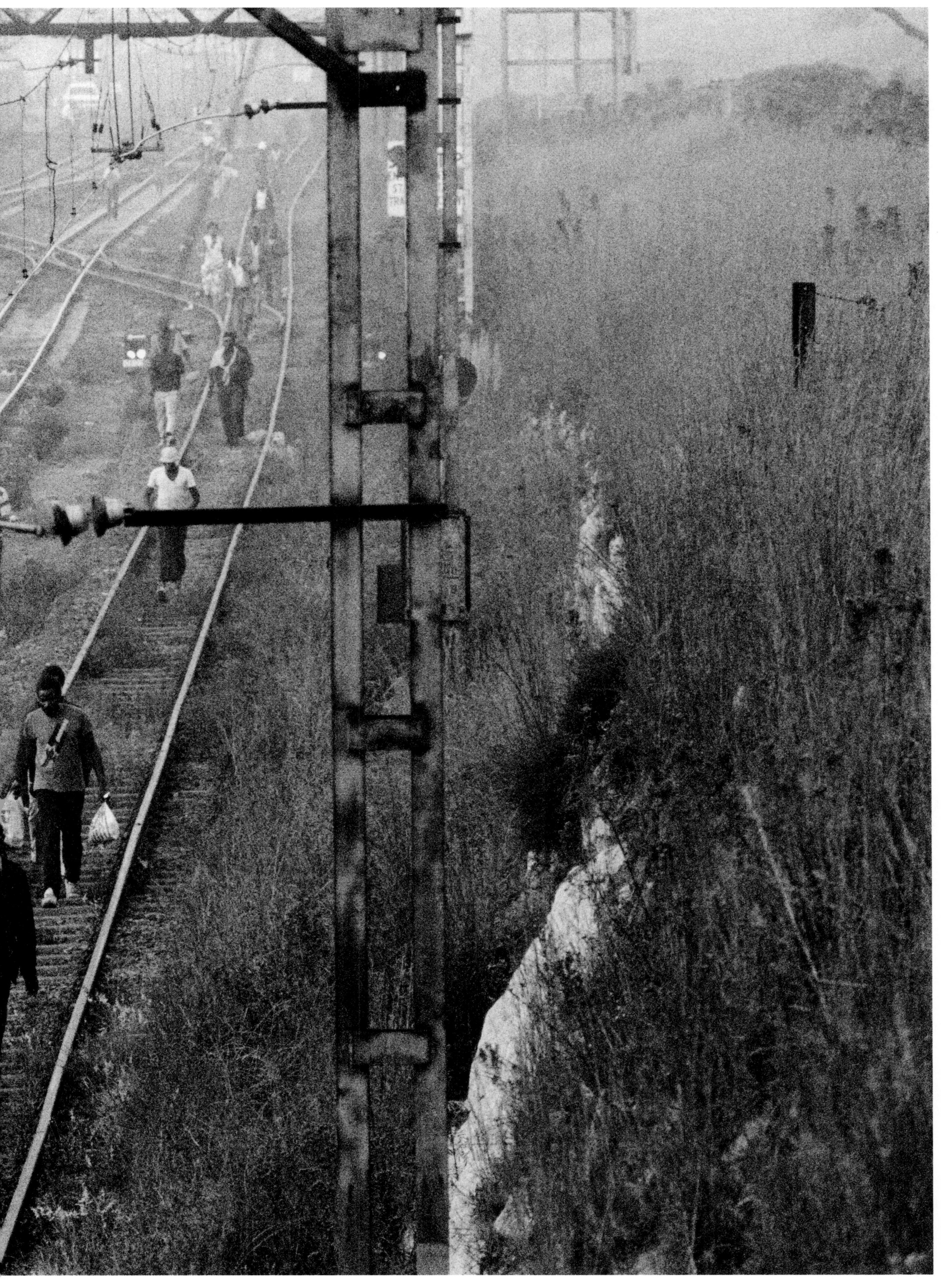

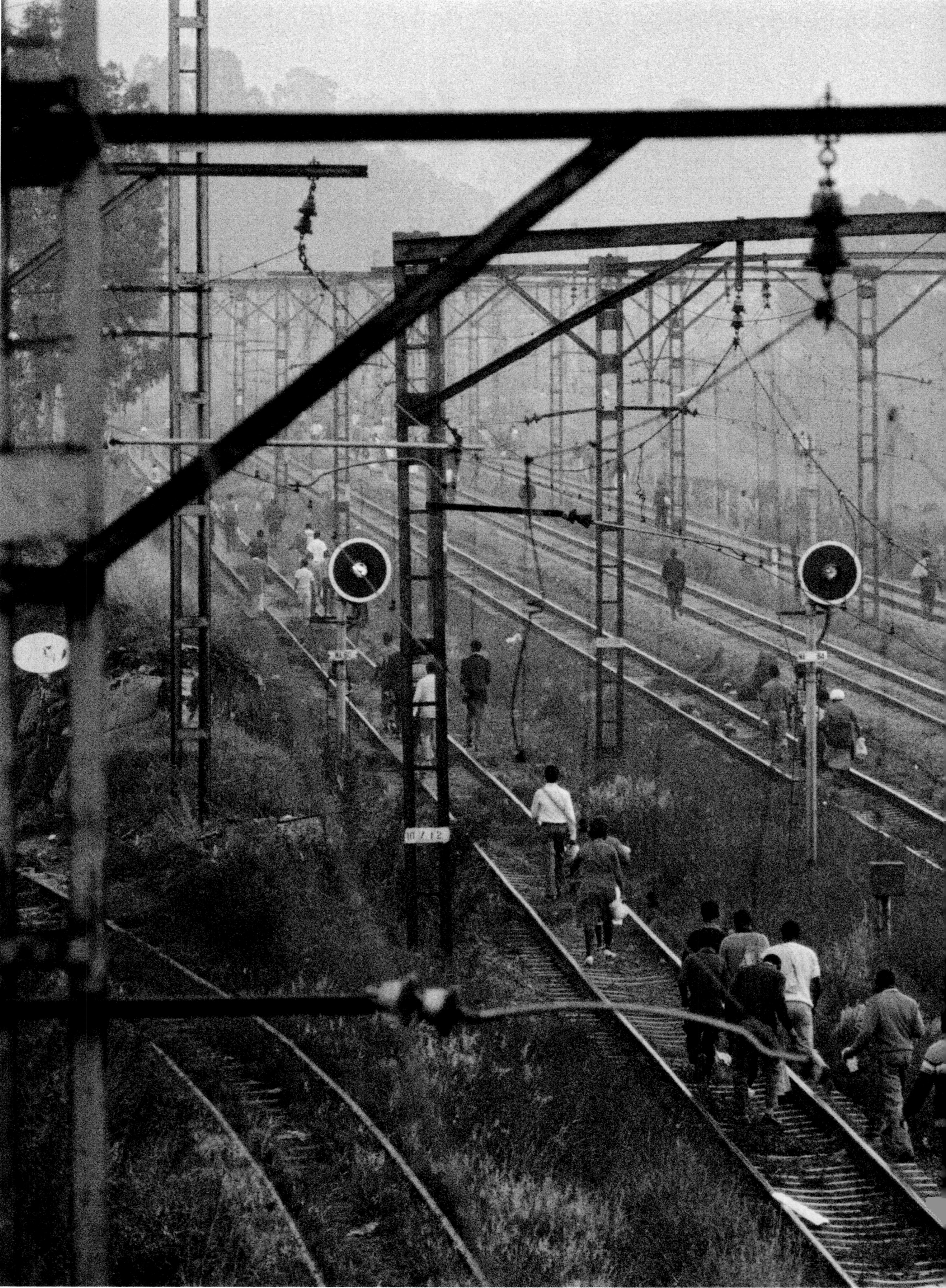

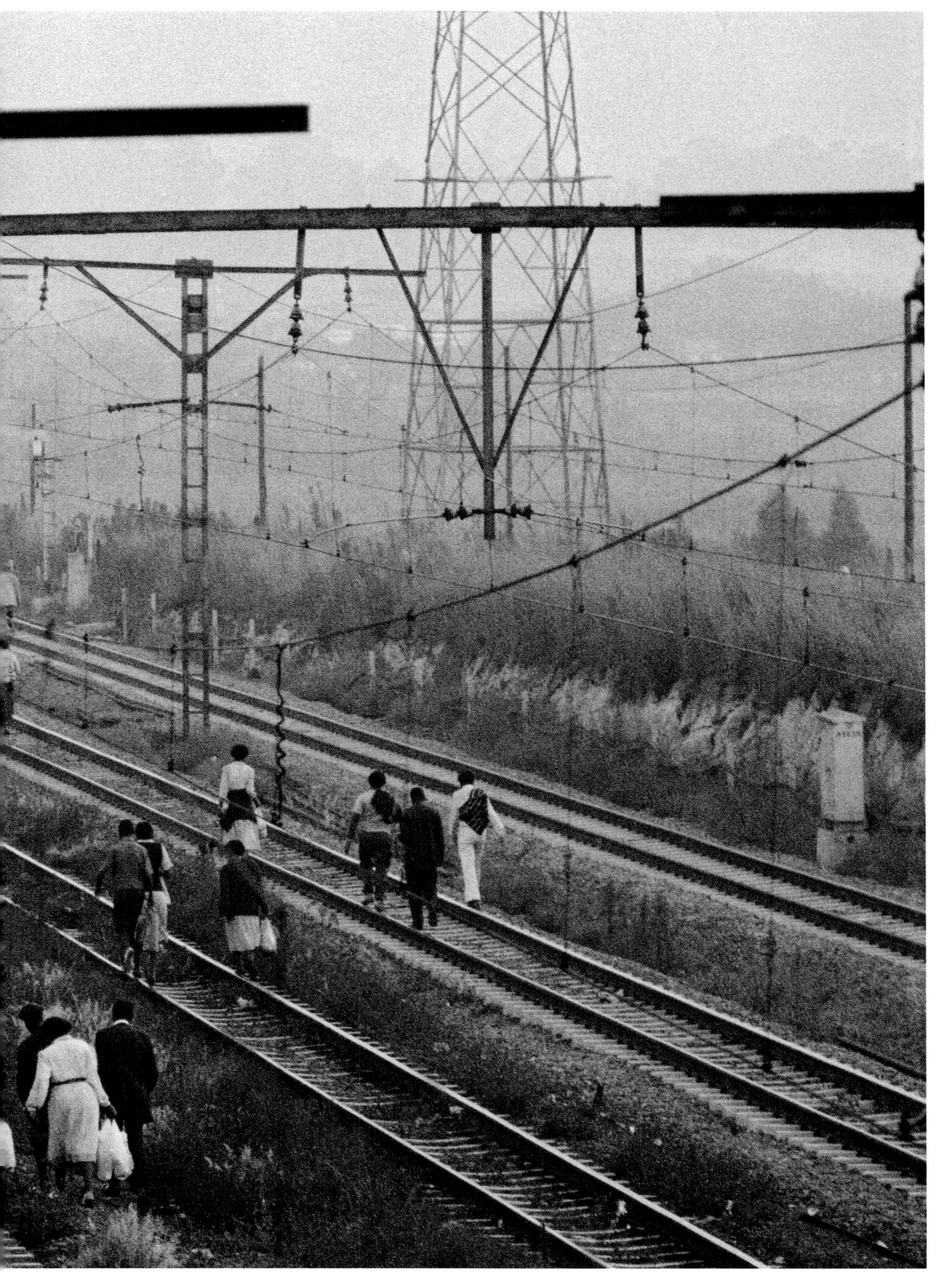

Santu Mofokeng: Stories
1—Train Church

Photographed over a few weeks in 1986
on the Soweto–Johannesburg commuter line

Collaboratively edited by Joshua Chuang
and Santu Mofokeng, with Lunetta Bartz

Special thanks to Mark McCain and Caro MacDonald,
Warren Siebrits and Lucia Duncan/MAKER

First edition published in 2015

© 2015 Santu Mofokeng for the images and text
© 2015 Steidl Publishers for this edition

Series concept: Joshua Chuang
Book design: Lunetta Bartz, Joshua Chuang
and Victor Balko/Steidl Design
Scans and separations by Steidl's digital darkroom
Production and printing: Steidl, Göttingen

Steidl
Düstere Straße 4
37073 Göttingen
Germany

Phone +49 551 49 60 60
Fax +49 551 49 60 649
mail@steidl.de
steidl.de

ISBN 978-3-86930-971-2
Printed in Germany by Steidl